Open Your Heart for Happy Relationships
10 Shift Keys

What Your Angels Have Been Trying to Tell You for Centuries

By

Eve Picquette

Illustrated by Alexandra Dan

Also by Eve Picquette

Mini Meditations – Shift Keys, Open Your Heart
Mini Meditations – Lighten Your Heart (series of 6)

You are invited to visit my author page - https://www.amazon.com/author/eve-advisorisin, Facebook at AdvisorIsIn and my page at AdvisorIsIn.com where I offer advice and techniques to help you open your heart for the happiest relationships and life, as well as Free Angel Readings and other gifts – click on Angel Messages!

COPYRIGHT 2012 by Eve Picquette

All rights reserved. No part of this book may be reproduced by any mechanical, photographic, or electronic process, or in the form of a recording, nor may it be stored in a retrieval system, transmitted, or otherwise be copied for public or private use—other than for "fair use" as brief quotations embodied in articles and reviews—without prior written permission of the author.

ISBN: 061569697X
ISBN 13: 9780615696973

Library of Congress Control Number: 2012916900
AdvisorIsIn, Enchanted Eve, Inc., Phoenix, Arizona.

*Dedicated to my lovely daughter Ashley Eden Benson,
the epitome of beauty on the inside and outside.
No one inspires us to search for answers in our own lives
more than do our children!*

*And to the Prayer attributed to St. Francis – whose principles I wanted
to live, but I could not figure out how....*

*Lord, make me an instrument of your peace.
Where there is hatred, let me sow love.
Where there is injury, pardon.
Where there is doubt, faith.
Where there is despair, hope.
Where there is darkness, light
Where there is sadness, joy...*

Contents

Shift Key 1.   Always Connect To Love 1

Shift Key 2.   Just Stop It, Really 9

Shift Key 3.   It's All About You 15

Shift Key 4.   It's Not About You 23

Shift Key 5.   Give Up On The Past 31

Shift Key 6.   Expect The Best Future 39

Shift Key 7.   Appreciate Everything Now 47

Shift Key 8.   Re-Choose Your Relationships 53

Shift Key 9.   Handle Conflict With Grace 61

Shift Key 10. Love So It Can Be Felt 69

♥ ♥ ♥

Preface

Using the 10 Shift Keys can help you to open your heart and create happier relationships. Our angels have been inspiring us with these keys for centuries—but many of us are slow learners.

- ❤ My angels knew what I needed all the time: I needed to open my heart to love. I knew all the reasons why—but I could not figure out *how*.
- ❤ The Shift Keys are the ten how-to-do-it ideas that opened my heart and shifted my life and relationships in the most profound way.
- ❤ There are only two reasons to make these shifts: you will feel lighter and happier, and you will attract that which is also lighter and happier—both will have a wonderful influence on your relationships.

As you read about the 10 Shift Keys, please remember:

- ❤ There is nothing new under the sun, and there are many paths to the same peace. These principles are timeless, and have been written about in many cultures and eras.
- ❤ You may notice that the Giver of unconditional love is undefined. The author knows the unconditional love, but cannot define the Giver.
- ❤ The keys will seem too simple; but they are not easy—that is why most people have not shifted their lives and relationships to love.
- ❤ You may find it challenging to take the action on these simple ideas, but if you do, the results will amaze you. There is hope, no matter what.
- ❤ You have an inner knowing that opens when you connect to love and light. You have angels – beings of unconditional love - who desire to help you.
- ❤ Do not believe anything or try anything unless it feels true for you. If it is true for you, the idea will make your heart feel lighter and happier.
- ❤ Open your heart and follow your deep knowing. You will be guided to the shifts that will "fix" your relationships and lighten your heart.

This book shares insights and processes that may assist the reader in dealing with common life experiences. This book is not intended to provide psychological, medical, financial, legal, or other professional services. If such assistance or counseling is needed, please contact a qualified counselor or other professional.

Introduction to the Angels - Hope

I believe that angels and the Giver of unconditional love - Creator of stars, galaxies and universal field -send us love, truth, and life energy all the time. In every age and every culture, truth has been and will be available to every seeker. Each chapter will be introduced by two of my angels of inspiration:

Hope – who stays aligned with my idea of angels—pure and bright and always loving.

Introduction to the Angels - Impatience

Angels are always there to inspire and remind us that the purpose of life is for joy—and for heaven's sake, stop taking it all so seriously, and have some fun!

Impatience – who—if she existed—has an edge, and really would like for some of us to get it together in this lifetime!

Shift Key 1: Always Connect to Love

Hope inspired, *Choose love over fear, and your heart will open to everything you want… —Unknown*

Impatience—if she existed—inspired, *What the world really needs is more love and less paperwork. —Pearl Bailey*

ou probably would like some magic stardust to change your life and your relationships. You may have been trying to live a loving, light hearted and happy life, but it has been less than a success. Perhaps you read something and decide to change. But you don't know exactly how and quickly fall back into the same patterns, just as I did. This book will give you practical shifts you can make in your life. I will be showing you what my angels of inspiration had been trying to show me for years: how to shift to love, open my heart, and have happier relationships. If you make these shifts, you will become more relaxed, have more fun, and draw in the very best from your relationships. You will have the magic stardust.

There are only two reasons to make these shifts:

- ♥ You will feel lighter and happier.
- ♥ You will attract people, places and events, which are also lighter and happier.

When you are feeling lighter and happier and have attracted the same, you will find that your relationships have evolved, as well. They will be fixed in amazing ways. The easiest way to explain this is to think about each of your relationships as a teeter-totter. You are on one end and your partner, boss, or friend is on the other end. When you shift to lighten your heart, it is like lightening the weight on your end of the teeter-totter. The person on the other end must change, as well. But you cannot control what choices the other person will make. Sometimes the other person may change in ways that are happy and pleasing and keep things in balance. Sometimes the other person will refuse to play and will move away from the relationship. If so, it will be OK. Because you are shifting your life to happiness and love—another partner, friend, or job will show up to take their place. They will have lighter hearts and be in balance with the changes you are making to lighten your heart and enjoy your life.

It would be nice to just ask your angels to sprinkle some stardust on all the difficult people in your life—swish! But, unfortunately, all those people have free choice, so you can only hope to influence them in a positive way. The very best way to influence the difficult people in your life is to connect to love, yourself. Whenever you are not feeling light and happy, just stop whatever you are doing or thinking and connect to love and ask for an open heart. When you do this, it will be like magic stardust for you—your vibration will raise, you will feel better, and this transformation will influence everyone around you in a positive way. The first Shift Key is learning that there is always magic stardust for you. You can always connect to love at any time, in any circumstance.

When I was learning this—I had it all backward. I wanted to get more love from others. But I did not have my own connection to love. I thought if I could change everyone else, I would be happy. As it turns out, I could not get anyone to change even one little bit. I had read many of the self-help books published in the last twenty-five years and become an authority on why I was sabotaging myself, and why my childhood or other experiences might be causing my pain. Everything I learned was helpful, but most of what I learned just made me want to change other people and circumstances beyond my control.

I also thought that working on my own education and accomplishments would make me more lovable and happy. I consistently chose with my head, then second-guessed my choices. I was accepted into medical school, and then chose not to attend. Later I became an attorney, not because I really wanted to be an attorney, but to make up for my "mistake" in not going to medical school. I was mostly concerned with how others would view me. My accomplishments were not from my heart. I am glad for all I accomplished as nothing we learn is ever wasted. But I was mostly operating out of worry and fear, not love.

I later found that I was making a major error and even though the results were poor – I didn't know what else to do.

- ♥ I had tried action to fix my life: working to change others and myself.
- ♥ I had tried asking for unconditional love to fix my life and relationships.

Neither worked well alone. I found happiness to be linked to both shifts in action and an open loving heart. First, I was trying so hard to do the right actions and be good enough – I wasn't really loving others or myself. Then, instead of moving on when a relationship, job or situation did not meet my needs – I thought I was being loving and I waited and waited – never taking action for myself, hoping that others would somehow change (despite strong evidence to the contrary!).

I wanted to stop wishing and hoping that others would change, so that I could be happy. I asked my angels to show me an answer: How could I love and respect myself and have harmonious and happy relationships, at the same time? This book contains the answers I found. The secret was to connect to love and then shift in the only areas where I had some control – my own thoughts, feelings and actions. When my own heart was right, then everyone and everything around me sorted out with the law of attraction. When I connected to love and my inner world (my heart) was right – so was my outer world.

Our angels have been trying to tell us this down through the ages. However, in the last few years, science is confirming the importance of connecting to love and its impact on our world. Joe Dispenza in his book, *Breaking the Habit of Being Yourself,* notes research indicating that we are each part of a vast, invisible field of energy, which actually responds to our thoughts and our feelings. We can use our minds and emotions to influence our reality. The neuroscientist, Dr. Newberg, in his book, *How God Changes Your Brain,* explains how just thinking of the word God and contemplative practices enhance the neural functioning of the brain in ways that improve physical and emotional health, no matter the religion or belief – as long as it is based on peace, love and compassion. The Institute of HeartMath research shows that positive thoughts actually add energy to our system and negative thoughts dissipate our energy. Our heart energy extends out three feet and more, influencing whatever is around us, as well as connecting to those we love.

Opening our hearts and feeling love, appreciation and compassion have a powerful beneficial effect on how we relate to life. I learned from Dr. David Hawkins's book, *Power versus Force,* that we all vibrate on an energy scale that ranges from low vibrations of despair, loneliness, and sadness up to the higher vibrations of hope, peace, happiness, and joy. Further, whatever level we are at determines what we attract—like attracts like.

- ♥ High vibrations —Happiness, Peace, and Joy
- ♥ On the way up —Hope, Expectation, and Contentment
- ♥ Low vibrations —Despair, Guilt, and Shame

Our emotions are based on how we interpret events and what we are thinking about. Our energy or vibration level is determined by the emotions we feel. Our vibration then determines what we attract and the outcome of our interactions with others and our world. So why don't we all just move up to joy? Usually because most of us grew up learning unhappy behaviors from our parents, who also wanted to live happy lives, but didn't know how. Unless we connect to love – it is difficult to break these unhappy patterns.

So no wonder I was not getting what I wanted! My attitude, emotions, and vibration were often fearful and worried or critical and negative. When I was critical and negative, that was the type of experience I was going to attract. I realized why the Law of Attraction wasn't working for me. I began to think of my thoughts as a flock of ducks flying through the sky. I could say some nice affirmations about what I wanted – that gave me three or four ducks going in the right direction. However, I had habitual thoughts and feelings of doubt, fear and unworthiness. Those twenty ducks were circling or going the wrong way, so chaos reigned. The universe responded not to my affirmations, but to my primary energy and vibration of fear and doubt. Law of attraction sounded good, if I could just stay in peace and joy – and attract that! But I didn't know how to shut off the anxious, negative perspective. I found that the easiest way was to simply ask for help and ask to be filled with the energy of unconditional love.

    I had signed up to go to an Angel Conference presented by Doreen Virtue, but was hesitant to go. My angels of inspiration knew I sincerely wanted help—when I ask I always get assistance. I usually recognize the angel's hand only in retrospect. But this time, I actually heard a voice in my heart say, "Atlanta, Atlanta." Since the conference was in Atlanta, that helped me find the courage to go. At that time Doreen had recorded a beautiful short meditation. I found the best way to get out of my negative thoughts was by listening to this. All I needed was a few minutes of quiet time. I felt the peace the first time I tried it. Later, if I found my thoughts drifting into negativity, I just paused a moment and asked for help again. I opened my heart to the energy of love and gratitude. I began connecting to light and love this way about fifteen years ago, and it has made a profound difference in my life.

    No matter what you are facing, connecting with the Gift of love and light in the universe (the power running the universe) will help. You may wonder how this will improve your relationships, but when you connect to the power of love, you can see yourself and others with a love that creates miracles. There is a power that spins the world and holds the stars and planets in place. That same power is available to you at all times. I do not mention religious words in this book, because many have unhappy feelings associated with religious names and symbols. I speak of the Gift and the Giver of unconditional love, because that is what I know. You can think of it as delivered by angels of unconditional love or the power that created the galaxies. It truly does not matter. It is light and love flowing to all of us, no matter what our belief or religion. The power is love, and it does not discriminate. You do not have to believe in it; all you have to do is hold out your hands. It keeps you alive, and you cannot turn it off. You can only temporarily cut off part of the flow—the part that would make you fully alive, vibrant, happy, and at peace.

    So your first Shift Key is to quiet your mind and open your heart. I want to emphasize—I am not recommending some formal meditation practice; often, just five minutes will move you up the emotional scale from fear to hope. The secret is not long meditation, but repeated requests throughout the day and a change in your emotions and vibration. You will receive help and see your situation with the eyes of love. If you ask, you will receive that magic stardust,

    When you walk in nature, listen to uplifting music; close your eyes and breathe slowly and deeply, your heart responds. When you ask for help from the Giver of love and life, or the angels of unconditional love, or when you repeat a comforting phrase, you are slowing down enough to notice and connect to the light and power of the universe. If you ask to be filled with the energy of unconditional love, you will feel your vibration rise, and you will feel better. If you are fearful or upset, you will become calmer. If you're angry or frustrated, you will move up to hope and see answers more clearly. It will help you with the rest of the Shift

Keys. It will raise your energy and vibration and make it more likely that you will attract what you want and reach your dreams. But even more important, it will connect you to love. You will see that everything, no matter how it appears, is really working out for you—right now.

You may be thinking that if that worked, it would be a miracle. It is.

Anyone Else Think This Is A Good Idea?

You are never alone or helpless. The force that guides the stars guides you too. —Anandamurti

Dwell on the beauty of life. Watch the stars, and see yourself running with them.
— Marcus Aurelius

If you want to find God, hang out in the space between your thoughts.
—Alan Cohen

Love stretches your heart and makes you big inside. —Margaret Walker

You don't have to go looking for love when it's where you come from. —Erhard

You are today where your thoughts brought you; you will be tomorrow where your thoughts take you. —James L. Allen

Everything that exists … is vibration in motion—and all of it is managed by the powerful *Law of Attraction*. —Abraham-Hicks

And my favorite:
If it weren't for my mind, my meditation would be excellent. —Ani Pema Chodron

Dare To Shift

Shift and connect to the energy of love and gratitude every single day. Put five to ten minutes on your calendar today. I cannot urge you more strongly—try it for a week and prove me wrong! I am not talking about long meditation – I believe that most of us are here to live our lives, rather than sit in contemplation. But we need to pause long enough to stop the negative thoughts and emotions, which are cutting off our supply of loving energy. We need to ask to be filled, here and now, with the energy of life, light and the power of love. We need to take the time to be lifted with the energy of love, to raise our vibration and open our hearts.

- ♥ If you feel you have no time, just take a few minutes in the car in a parking lot. I have done some of my best connection in the car, or waiting for an appointment in a place where I could close my eyes and relax. If I am in a really stressful situation, I excuse myself for just five minutes (even if I have to retreat to the restroom). I breathe deeply and ask for calm and clarity or whatever I need. I see myself breathing in love, and ask to be filled with light and to see the situation with love. This has helped me respond and make decisions in a clear and positive way.
- ♥ Close your eyes, breathe slowly and deeply and repeat a soothing phrase. I like the phrase *All is well*. If you are alone, this Brain Gym exercise is very relaxing: Cross your ankles, stretch out your arms, put the back of your hands together, move the left over the right and clasp your hands, bringing your clasped hands under and up, resting on your heart. If you have time, you can use a short meditation or soothing music without words.
- ♥ Ignore any negative thoughts or your to-do list—repeat your request to be flooded with the stardust of unconditional love and light. Continue relaxing, breathing slowly.
- ♥ Once you feel some sense of peace, if you want, you can also ask for specific help. You can ask for clarity on a problem at work; the ability to see your partner or children with more loving eyes; or the ability to see your own goals clearly, without worrying about everyone else. Then let it go, and continue the day.
- ♥ Do not ask for predictions on the future, because both you and others have free choice. You can choose again at any time, and change your future. The angels of inspiration do not predict the future, but angel messengers of unconditional love or the love and light of the universe can help you recognize what makes you light and happy and help you move toward the best next step for you. So ask to clearly know in your heart what choice will bring you and others the most love and happiness now.
- ♥ Note – This is asking for help in living your life, as you move toward the good things you have chosen. This is not about channeling, predicting the future, asking for someone to make choices for you, or connecting with anything other than the pure light of unconditional love. The Giver of unconditional love and light only wants you to choose and will help you follow your choices –Giver of unconditional love, or angels of unconditional love never dictate your path, you have free choice. But connecting to love will lighten any path you choose, increasing your freedom and joy.
- ♥ Only choose loving thoughts that lighten your heart. If a thought makes you feel heavy or burdened, it is a lie. Ignore it and expect positive inspiration later. Ask to be raised above critical vibration.

See all negative thoughts fade away with the stardust of love. Ask to connect to the loving truth of unconditional love and that loving truth will make you feel light and free.

- ♥ Note: Sometimes you will know that you must do something, like apologize, that you don't want to do – but thinking of completing that task will lighten your heart with relief and you will feel that it is right and true. Sometimes what is best for you won't make everyone else happy, but it will make your heart lighter.
- ♥ You will receive help. You may get an immediate thought or idea when you ask and open your heart to unconditional love—or, at a later time, you will hear a song or snippet of conversation, speak with someone, or find a book or magazine article that seems meant to open your eyes to new possibilities or gives you a new insight. But remember – if it is the true direction for you – it will make you feel lighter and happier – not burdened, guilty or fearful. Your inner knowing is from light and love – learn to trust it.

What Will I Get Out Of This?

Purpose and Peace

When I first moved to Arizona, I had a job I enjoyed and was living the life I thought I wanted, but life still felt like a daily struggle. I decided to make the drive to work a sort of prayer for help and an appreciation of my blessings. I repeated soothing phrases, over and over, asking my angels of inspiration and the Giver of unconditional love and light to lift my energy and give me the grace to enjoy the day and bring good to all I met. By the time I got to work, I was feeling a sense of purpose and a light heart, ready to face the day. I had connected with love and begun to understand that the connection to love, not any external events, was what made me happy.

Clarity

I wanted to find an interesting program for my daughter when she was going through some difficult experiences. I asked for help, and within a few days I got it. On a flight for a conference, I was seated right next to a woman who was part of an organization that did wonderful weekend programs for teenagers. She was able to tell me all about the program. I took my daughter to this weekend program in Seattle the next week. It was a life-changing event and helped her to come to terms with some of the unhappy things in her life, such as the recent death of her great-grandfather. I knew I had connected to love and had received a wonderful answer.

Deep Happiness

You are *so* loved, and you will find that when you connect to love, you can feel happiness and peace, no matter what is happening around you. This will help you see your relationships with eyes of love and respond to your partner, family, and friends from a stronger, happier, heart-centered place. You will begin to expect blessings and miracles. You will see the difference in how you relate to everyone when first you open your heart and connect to love.

Childre, D. (1999) The HeartMath Solution, NY HarperCollins
Dispenza, J. (2013) *Breaking the Habit of Being Yourself: How to Lose Your Mind and Create a New One*, Hay House
Dyer, W. (2012) *I Am: Wishes Fulfilled* (CD)
Newberg, A., Waldman, M. (2010) *How God Changes Your Brain, Breakthrough Findings from a Leading Neuroscientist*, NY, Random House
Schmidt, J. (2003) *Still, Still, Still* MP3
Tabell, R. (2012) *The Lord's Prayer* MP3
Picquette, E. (2012) "Connecting to Love," track on *Mini Meditation—Shift Keys* MP3
Virtue, D. (2004) *Chakra Clearing* (book and CD)
For an easy click on book list of all the reference books – go to <u>AdvisorIsIn.com</u>

Shift Key 2: Just Stop It, Really

Hope inspired, Never let life's hardships disturb you ... no one can avoid problems, not even saints or sages.—Nichiren Daishonin

Impatience—if she existed — inspired, Man invented language to satisfy his deep need to complain. —Lily Tomlin

hifting to kindness and acceptance in Shift Key 2 will make a major difference in your life and your relationships. Just this one shift—stopping complaints and criticism—will lighten your heart. How can you feel happy if you are concentrating on everything that is wrong? You will find that you can get much of what you want without making anyone wrong—including yourself. This is so simple— but complaining and blaming is such a habit, it can be difficult to make the shift to seeing everything with positive regard, kindness, and acceptance. I don't know why I complained for so long. Though I have done an inordinate amount of it, I have *never* found complaining or blaming helped me, at all. What about you? Did you ever really get happier relationships and encounters by complaining or blaming? If not, then you can shift to accepting what you can't change, anyway. Your partner, family, and friends will feel more affection for you when you stop criticizing and blaming over things you cannot change. In addition, when you stop you no longer attract blame and criticism of you—which is a lovely result!

This one was a big shift for me. My angels were probably relieved when I began to make this shift, since complaining and blaming kept me in a vibration far from peace and love. I always felt like I was a good, kind

person and didn't deserve some of the tough times I had in life. Since I was not brave enough to do much direct confrontation, blaming, or criticizing, this added to my self-righteous feeling that I didn't deserve any problems. However, I blamed and complained in my mind, sometimes mulling things over and feeling hurt for hours and days. I usually could not see my contribution to my problems and didn't realize it affected my energy. I just didn't know why these things kept happening to me. One day, when I was finally open enough to see myself, the angels gave me some clarity.

- ♥ I realized that I was critical a lot, particularly at work. I could usually see a better way to do things and made comments to other observers. Since I was not directing my comments at the person or department doing the job, I didn't think it was much of a problem. After all, I was being helpful and giving constructive criticism.
- ♥ I gave unwanted advice and "helpful suggestions"—particularly to my daughter. I thought I was helping, but my angels led me to read a book that made it clear that unwanted advice felt like criticism to her—and kept us from being as close. What a concept! I don't know why I didn't get it before, as I certainly didn't like it when others gave me advice. I always feel criticized, even if it is constructive!

I was also aware that complaining wasn't a good thing, but I never realized how much I did, and the real implications for me. Once again the law of attraction broke through my illusion that it was OK to constructively complain or blame. It took me awhile—until I realized:

- ♥ If I criticized or blamed someone else, I attracted criticism of what I was doing and myself (and, unfortunately, I had the experiences to prove it).
- ♥ If I complained that someone had taken advantage, I was staying in vulnerable, sad feelings. My vibration and energy would match and attract people who were also feeling small and vulnerable, but felt better when they attacked and bullied someone.
- ♥ If I offered unwanted advice or suggestions at work or to people I loved, it might feel like criticism to them and push them away, preventing the very closeness I wanted most.

So I knew I had to stop. I had to shift, because complaining and blaming attracted more of the same—and I didn't want it! It kept me in a vibration far away from happiness, love, and peace.

Naturally you have human emotions, and sometimes it is normal to feel anger, blame, and other negative emotion. You will hurt only yourself if you stuff or suppress your feelings. So when life shows up, how can you feel and then resolve the feelings quickly, and avoid wallowing in or spreading the negativity?

- ♥ Try the exercises in the Dare to Shift section below to release your negative feelings.
- ♥ For abuse, serious family conflict, loss, or divorce—of course you will need to go over the situation with someone. You need to be heard and understood, and a counselor or minister can help. However, once you have been heard, do your best to move on and begin working on the solution.
- ♥ Continued repeating of sad or angry history will keep you identifying and attracting more misery. Find a counselor that will help you build your future, and ask good questions. What have you learned about yourself? What can you do to move on and make your life excellent, no matter what anyone else did or what happened in the past?

This process will lighten your heart. You will become the delightful person who takes life more lightly. You probably appreciate people who take care of themselves and are willing to let supposed slights and inconveniences go. You likely know someone who can see their part in any conflict and is willing to apologize for their part and give others the benefit of the doubt.

Be that someone, and make yourself a complaint-and blame-free zone! Keep it up, and you will start to attract less blame and criticism and more peace. Try it. It will move you up the emotional scale toward happiness and you will like the results.

Anyone Else Think This Is A Good Idea?

Any fool can criticize, condemn and complain and most fools do. —Benjamin Franklin

Untold suffering seldom is. —Franklin P. Jones

Keep your face to the sunshine and you will not see the shadows. —Helen Keller

Small-minded people blame others. Average people blame themselves. The wise see all blame as foolishness. —Epictetus

Change your thoughts and change your world. —Norman Vincent Peale

I have yet to find the man, however exalted his station, who did not do better work and put forth greater effort under a spirit of approval than under a spirit of criticism. —Charles Schwab

The measure of a truly great man is the courtesy with which he treats lesser men. —Anonymous

My favorite:
I've eaten things that didn't complain this much. —Denis Leary

Dare To Shift

First—just stop it! Observe yourself today and see how often you criticize or complain about anything: the traffic, the grocery line, drivers, your boss, politics, the government, and more. Know that when you complain and blame, you are drawing more of the same right toward you. I found it helpful to think of complaints in light of the Serenity Prayer: "God grant me the serenity to accept the things I cannot change; courage to change the things I can; and wisdom to know the difference." (In short, I can fix what is mine and shut up about the rest.) Oh, and neither one requires me to express myself by complaining or blaming!

Next, if you are still tempted to complain or criticize, ask yourself if talking about this will make you or anyone else feel lighter or happier? If not, shift and turn it around! Whenever anything negative gets your attention, ask yourself if you want more of those things about which you are complaining? If not – start thinking of what you do want or something that you can appreciate. This invites the universe to help and opens you to something more positive. If the situation seems negative, asking this question will usually lighten your mood and your vibration and allow something better. This, again, may sound too simple; but it will change your energy and move you toward looking for help and solutions rather than staying in the negative energy of the problem. Just this shift can create miracles in your life. At the end of each day, give yourself credit for every time you are able to turn a complaint or blame statement into – *I open my heart to a better solution, please help.*

Third, for difficult or ongoing conflicts or irritants, you may need to release your feelings. Try writing about it on a piece of paper, using three steps:

- What is the problem and why is it *so* upsetting? Let it all out!
- What do you wish were different? What would you like to have happen or to have happened in the past?
- Is there anything you need to correct or for which you should apologize? (Of course it is their fault, but did you have a part? If you did, take care of your part now and it will give you some immediate relief! Did you learn anything? Is there any action you can take so that it will be better for you if this kind of situation happened again?)

Tear up or shred the paper in a satisfying way. (Don't neglect this part—your goal is to handle this without causing more negativity for yourself or others—using a computer is not recommended!) Finally, ask the universe or the angels of unconditional love to lift away the negative feelings. I like to take a deep breath and visualize blowing the anger or sadness away or blowing it up with great visual fireworks.

Finally, use a gift list to switch your energy to positive. Whenever you feel like complaining or criticizing—instead, shift your thoughts and think up something for your "gift" list. Decide to give a "gift" to someone every day—someone who is not expecting it. Just planning this little gift can change your outlook and lift your mood. The gift does not have to be money or cost money—but it can, if you want. Some examples: Send a sincere e-mail complimenting someone at work who could use a lift. Buy a small bouquet or miniature box of candy to surprise someone. Look a clerk or service person in the eye, and really express your appreciation. Decide to compliment your partner or children in some way today, no matter how annoying they may have been. Try this, and you will be surprised at how it lifts your heart and affects everyone around you.

If you have a major sadness or anger in your life, see Shift Key 5 on letting go of the past and processes such as Emotional Freedom Technique (EFT). And don't forget to connect to love for a few minutes every day, as it is the most important shift of all!

What Will I Get Out Of This?

Your family will thank you, your partner will thank you, your co-workers will thank you. No, really. You may not get any thanks, but you will feel better about yourself and improve everyone's experience, including your own!

Directly ask for what you want, but don't criticize or blame anyone. This will raise your vibration (and, incidentally, that of everyone around you):

- ♥ It will immediately improve your self-esteem, as you take responsibility for yourself. Indulging in a fit of sulks or anger may temporarily relieve your feelings, but in the long term it never feels good to be a victim or to allow yourself to be at someone else's mercy.
- ♥ It will also improve your relationships. When you are negative, angry, complaining and blaming, you influence everyone around you, and everyone has less contentment. Instead, if you bring peace with you, people will be glad to see you and happy to know you.
- ♥ Your relationships will also improve when you stop offering unasked-for advice and just offer encouragement and support. My relationship with my daughter greatly improved when I started letting her live her life in her own way. She wanted to be around a noncritical mother who offered love and support to her—just as she is.
- ♥ But really, the best reason to shift your behavior is the law of attraction. If you are blaming, you attract situations and people that will give you more of what you are talking or thinking about. Ever noticed that when one thing goes wrong, it keeps getting worse, until you finally give up and let it go? That's the law of attraction at work. When you finally finish blaming and complaining, only then can things get better.

I had a great example of this a few years ago. I was on a long drive with a friend who always gets up on the right side of the bed in the morning and exudes positive energy. I enjoy being in her happy energy and any positive feelings I have seem to be multiplied in her presence. I was aware of this, but didn't realize exactly why.

On that day, we decided to pass the time by giving each other a little history of our lives: where we went to school, how we met our husbands, what jobs we had held over the years. She began to talk first. She briefly mentioned a first marriage that sounded emotionally painful. She also mentioned, in passing, a major injury. But there was no complaining or blaming anyone. She didn't even blame herself, or talk about how she should have done things differently. (Once one of my favorite themes.) Those were just the facts, and she concentrated on the positive. She found the strength to walk out of the marriage. She had later found the love of her life and had a happy second marriage. Everything was good, and there was no complaining, no blaming, and no drama.

Then it was my turn. I had a major aha moment. I could lament some of my regrettable choices or sad events. Or I could—like my friend—talk about the positive in my history. I could mention that I was blessed to get a scholarship for college and that I had numerous good breaks and advancements in my career. I had a choice—I could talk negatively about my relationships, or I could mention how much I learned and gained. I could talk about my mistakes (they are many) or about all that I had been given. I decided to make a shift that day. Now whenever I am asked about my past or even my present, I make a studied effort to talk about all the blessings and favors I have received. The more I talk about my blessings, the more I notice them and the more I receive. I am sure my friends heave a sigh of relief! Try this for yourself—you will feel so much lighter and happier when you do.

Recommended Resources You Might Enjoy

Bowen, W. (2007) *A Complaint Free World*. UK, Random House.
Dyer, W. (2011) *Excuses Begone! How to Change Lifelong, Self-Defeating Thinking Habits,* Hay House, NY
For humorous inspiration—see YouTube clip of Bob Newhart sketch "Stop It", http://youtu.be/y8Et28kBi1A
Lipton, B. (2013) *The Honeymoon Effect, The Science of Creating Heaven on Earth* Hay House, NY
Winget, L. (2004) *Shut Up, Stop Whining & Get a Life*, John Wiley and Sons.
For an easy click on book list of all the reference books – go to AdvisorIsIn.com

Shift Key 3: It's All About You

Hope inspired, *Yesterday I was clever, so I wanted to change the world. Today I am wise, so I am changing myself.*
—Rumi

Impatience—if she existed—inspired, *Do not marry a man to reform him. That is what reform schools are for.*
—Mae West

he 3rd Shift Key will lighten your heart and shift another big weight off your end of the relationship teeter-totter. This shift will help you stop wasting all the energy you are spending trying to change things over which you have absolutely no control. It is a heavy burden to carry when you think it is up to you to change everyone. You can drop that burden right now, and focus your energy on some place where it will do some good! If you are like me, you have been spending too much energy in the wrong places. You can learn to put the focus on changing your circumstances to give yourself more of what you want, instead of spending your precious time trying to persuade others to do what you want. You can let go of everything that doesn't directly impact you and set clear boundaries and consequences for the few things that do. You can arrange your life to have many of the things that you are waiting for others to give.

If angels became weary, mine would have been exhausted waiting for me to realize what I was doing. I expected others to make me happy. I also spent time doing for others, secretly hoping they would respond and want to do something to please me. I was often disappointed. When I began to understand more about the law of attraction, I discovered that the universe does not guarantee that if we are good enough, a particular person or event will appear or do what we want. Despite what I wanted, the universe does not take away someone else's personal choice in order to please me. For example, I may not get the exact boyfriend I want, because he has freedom of choice (thank goodness)! But if I shift, my peaceful energy and vibration will attract more things that give me happiness—and, in the end, the loving relationships I want.

Over a long period, I learned to focus on my own attitude, and myself, if I wanted to feel happier. It was a big shift to stop thinking that others should change to make me happier. I remember many occasions when I spoiled my own good times. I would be at the lake having a good time, and I would begin thinking about some supposed injustice or unhappy event: thoughts like the fact that my friends had partners who bought them nice presents and surprises, while mine usually asked something like, "I guess it is your birthday—what do you want to do?" I concentrated on who didn't do what I needed. I just didn't see that I could have planned a fun dinner out, if that was what I desired. I could have changed things to suit myself and had as much birthday fuss as I wanted. Instead, I waited for someone else to do something I wanted—I ruined my own day. And to top it off—even with all my negative thoughts or complaints—I still didn't manage to change anyone else!

I had been taught that if you were unselfish, you would do what others wanted. So I tried to do what everyone wanted me to do—and then I was sad or upset if others (selfishly, I felt) did what they wanted for themselves. What a circular disaster! I was listening to an Abraham-Hicks CD on the law of attraction and I heard a description that finally made it all clear to me—or maybe my angels tapped me on the head. Anyway, I finally got the point.

- ♥ It is not selfish to take care of yourself and do the things you want to do in life.
- ♥ Real selfishness is expecting/insisting that others to do what you want them to do.

It was distressing to admit, but also—what a relief! I had to see that when I expected others to do what I wanted them to do, I was the one who was selfish.

Have you ever waited for someone to give you what you could have obtained for yourself? Have you missed any good times because you didn't have a friend who wanted to go to an event? Have you ever felt that you could be really happy, if everyone around you would change? If others would treat you fairly, take responsibility, do the "right" things, and treat you kindly—then you could be happy? There is bad news and good news.

- ♥ The bad news is that no matter how much you wish or how hard you try—*no one else* is going to really change to please you.
- ♥ The good news is that you can change to please you, and if you do, others will have to change, one way or another.

It is like a teeter-totter. If you change things on your end, it can't help but change what happens on the other end.

There is a variation to this idea of changing others that is just as futile—you may think your mate, boss, or friends are doing something destructive, and they should change, not for you, but for their own good. Still, it is a hopeless, futile exercise, and will ruin the harmony and peace in your relationships. If the behavior of adults does not directly affect your daily living, you must let it go. You can only change yourself, no one else.

- ♥ They may need to experience the results of their behavior multiple times to decide to change.
- ♥ They may change in a wonderful way that you never thought of or expected
- ♥ They may never change, and it has to be OK—you cannot let their behavior determine whether you enjoy all there is to appreciate in your life.

However, if the behavior of your mate, boss, or friends directly affects your life, of course you can set boundaries that keep you safe and happy. But the boundaries must be about you and what you will expect and tolerate, and must not be focused on changing them.

Right up there with wanting to change your mate, you may also be spending a lot of energy trying to mold and change your children. Have you tried to explain what you want, ask for them to study more, wear different clothes, come home on time? *Has that worked?* Yet you may try it again and again—lecturing, reminding, asking, pleading. This can increase everyone's frustration and unhappiness. It might be worth it, if it worked, but it does not. See the good news and bad news above.

You might agree that maybe you could let go of some of the rules (that are being ignored anyway) and have more peace at home, but what if your kids are doing things that really impact your daily life? You cannot change the basic personality and make-up of your children, but that doesn't mean you don't have rights as parents. Again, the focus needs to be on you—what you need and how your children's actions impact your life. By defining what you want for yourself, you can change. You can know firmly what you can tolerate, and you can set boundaries that make your life better.

Anyone Else Think This Is A Good Idea?

The best sermons are lived, not preached. —Cowboy Wisdom

A man asked his mother, "How can I find the right woman for me?" She answered, "Don't worry about finding the right woman—concentrate on becoming the right man." —Unknown

Life is 10 percent what you make it and 90 percent how you take it. —Irving Berlin

It's not what happens to you, but how you react to it that matters. —Epictetus

The Universe is not punishing you or blessing you. The Universe is responding to the vibrational attitude that you are emitting. The more joyful you are, the more Well-being flows to you—and you get to choose the details of how it flows. —Abraham-Hicks

Hold yourself responsible for a higher standard than anybody else expects of you. —Henry Ward Beecher

My favorite:
A positive attitude may not solve all your problems, but it will annoy enough people to make it worth the effort. —Herm Albright

Dare To Shift

Shift your focus from others back to yourself. How can you arrange your life to have what you want, without manipulating or expecting others to meet your expectations? Give up your expectations that others will change—give up lecturing, begging, pleading, raging, anger or tears. You don't have to try that any more—feel your heart lighten! You are going to increase your own peace and happiness by accepting what does not directly impact you, and setting clear measurable boundaries for what does.

Shift boundaries for mates, bosses, and friends

Make sure this really affects you, and is not just a desire to control.

- ♥ Ask yourself if the issue is really important to your happiness and peace.
- ♥ If so, make a list of one or two important issues. Note on the list why they affect you and how they make you feel.
- ♥ Go over the list with your partner or friend at a time when you are both relatively relaxed.
- ♥ Start by stating how important the relationship is to you and how much you appreciate this person and the relationship. Make a promise to yourself that you won't accuse, attack, or go over past wrongs.
- ♥ Simply state what you want and need and particularly why—the why must be *only* because of how it makes you feel to have or not have it (not your partner's or friend's need to change). You must stay in the feeling.

- Then state what you will do for yourself (without blaming your partner or friend) if your need is not met. Set only consequences for which you are prepared to follow through.

Shift boundaries for children and teenagers

Again, before you take any action, make sure that this really affects you, and is not just an opinion, matter of taste, or generation gap. Do not bother with minor irritants—you just don't like your children's choice of sports, dress, or what they like to eat or leave on their plates. Let them choose as much as you can! Spend most of your time with your children looking for the good and lovable, and point it out with praise and affection. Give positive, age-appropriate hugs and affection. Set rules only for things that are truly important.

- If their behavior is about them, intervene only if their choice violates a real health issue, safety issue, criminal law, or a serious value such as honesty, integrity, or cleanliness.
- If the behavior infringes on your rights to a peaceful home, free of fighting, disorder, loud music, or lack of respect, then decide what you can accept.
- Ask yourself, Will this be important a year from now? If so, set boundaries, if not, consider letting it go.
- Pick only a few major concerns. You have only so much energy!
- Sit down with pen and paper and set your positive boundaries: what you *want* and can accept, and *why* it is important.
- Set a time to talk with your children. Express how the issue affects you and the household—don't accuse or attack your children or teenagers.
- Post the rules and consequences. It must be easy and clear to everyone whether the rule is followed or not—do not make your life harder!
- The consequence should be realistic and easy to enforce or withhold—do not make your life harder!

Consistency is key—always follow through with consequences, or the boundary is useless. And don't forget to connect to love for a few minutes every day, as it is the most important shift of all!

What Will I Get Out Of This?

Your children and partners will be clear about what you want and what you will do to protect your own happiness. There will be a lot more peace. You have to express yourself only once—and post the boundaries for children and teenagers. You will feel free to take the actions that make your life better, as everyone is clear about what you expect. You won't need to blame or complain, because you are making sure to get important things that you want in your life. When you take care of yourself, you will get more respect.

Examples of boundaries and guidelines that have worked for me, or for people I know

Boundaries with heart, for adults:

- ♥ To a partner—I would love to have you to go to the play with me on Saturday night. I know it is not your favorite, so if you don't want to go, please let me know, and I will see if my best friend can go. I don't want to miss the performance!
- ♥ To parent—When you criticize my partner, it feels like a judgment of my choices and makes us both uncomfortable. In the future, if that happens, we will plan to leave.

Boundaries with heart—for children:

- ♥ I need you to call when you get home from school. ("Why?") When you don't call, I worry about your safety.
- ♥ I need to hear courtesy and respect for family members. ("Why?") When I hear you say mean things about each other, I know you are hurting each other's hearts.

Boundaries with heart—for teenagers:

- ♥ Ignore the negative, don't even comment, unless it is part of a set of written boundaries. You will be amazed at the peace you will have if you praise what you love and just ignore everything else your teenager does, unless it is truly a major issue.

- Set boundaries with clear consequences. Let them choose as much as you can, and let them know you love them no matter what they choose. At this age, if it is really important to them, they likely will hide their activity, and do it anyway.
- Set only a few boundaries—tied to curfew, participation in school, safety, and respect and courtesy to others in the home.
- The *why* of rules must be tied to real reasons of safety, health, legal, or respect—not just your opinion of their friends, clothing, career choice, or eating habits!
- The consequences must be tied to something that the teenager desires and that can be withheld easily—like having a car or use of a car, or reward of a dollar amount to spend for clothing or a trip. Keep it simple and measurable. Remember this is to take care of you—don't make life harder for you.

Recommended Resources You Might Enjoy

Jeffers, S. (2006) *Feel the Fear…and Do It Anyway*. Ballantine.

———. (2001) *I'm OK, You're A Brat!: Setting the Priorities Straight and Freeing You From the Guilt and Mad Myths of Parenthood*. Los Angeles: Renaissance Books.

Latham, G. (1990) *The Power of Positive Parenting*. Utah: P & T Ink.

Norwood, R. (2008) *Women Who Love Too Much: When You Keep Wishing and Hoping He'll Change*. New York: Pocket Books

Picquette, E. (2012) "Heart Blessings" on *Mini Meditation—Shift Keys*, MP3 available for download.

Picquette, E. (2012) "About Children" and, "About Teenagers" on *Mini Meditation—Lighten Your Heart—* MP3 available for download.

For an easy click on book list of all the reference books – go to AdvisorIsIn.com

Shift Key 4: It's Not About You

Hope inspired, *I care not what others think of what I do, but I care very much about what I think of what I do!* — Theodore Roosevelt

Impatience—if she existed—inspired, *Man was created a little lower than the angels, and has been getting lower ever since.* —Josh Billings

his should be a relief: Shift Key 4 is *not* about you! It's about learning to accept those annoying other people and how they treat you! This is another area that will lift your spirits, raise your vibration, and lighten your heart, if you let it. When you let others have their unhappy experiences, and finally know that it is (most often) not about you, life is better. It also takes pressure off your partners and friends, which will improve your relationships all around. It will be a relief when you can really accept that whatever other people do or say is probably not about you. Your head knows this, but in your heart you may still take things personally. If another's behavior is particularly hurtful, you can also do an exercise that will help you see what partners and friends are in your best interest.

    I know I spent years feeling that every slight—every unreturned phone call, everyone who failed to return my smile—was either my fault or at least directed toward me. I was relieved when I realized that there might be something else going on in the other person's world that had nothing to do with me. Of course I should have known better! One time I felt hurt for days, when I thought I had not been invited to a friend's party. It turned out that my friend's mother was ill, and my friend had left town unexpectedly and never invited anyone. I wasted time feeling hurt and left out of … nothing.

I have since learned to (usually) shift and let it go. If I find myself on the way to feeling hurt or left out, I can usually stop the slide by deciding that there is a good reason I didn't get what I desired—maybe something better will happen, I will meet someone new, or I will plan something even more fun to do! I decided I had spent way too much time and energy mulling over every remark, nuance, and gesture and being angry or hurt that things didn't go my way. Instead I could choose to give the person or situation and myself the benefit of compassion. I didn't have to take anything personally. Whatever happens really might not be directed toward me, or about me. Sometimes it may take some effort, but if I can stay positive, I can expect the universe to bring something even better into my life, whether that is a missed party or a missing love relationship.

Another thing I learned is that not all my thoughts are mine. Sometimes I am picking up other people's thoughts and worries and making them my own. If you are having a negative feeling, consider the following:

- ♥ You might ask yourself, *Is this how I feel, or am I picking up something near me?* You could be absorbing the anger, fear, and upset of the people around you. Maybe it is your mother-in-law, who is really upset about what the children are doing, and not you? Maybe it is the talk-show host who is so upset about the cost of gas, or what the government is or is not doing and you are just taking on their feelings!
- ♥ Ask the question. If it is not your thought or feeling, you will immediately feel better and can just move on with your day. You won't need to waste any time on something that is not your primary concern.

However, sometimes there are events that seem too negative to ignore. You may find yourself reacting to negative events and people by either being angry or feeling hurt. You might be angry that someone else was angry or took advantage. Or you might feel hurt that someone could be so unkind to you. In your interpersonal relationships, you may want to ask yourself if there was anything you did for which you should make amends in the situation. If so, then you may want to apologize for anything that is your part, and let it go. If everything you do does not work, and you continue to feel that a relationship is hurtful or abusive, you will need to decide if you want to continue to be friends, work in that job, or continue to see that person.

I have left positions several times in my career because I was spending too much time trying to stay happy in a job where I felt I had done my best, but just wasn't a fit. I have also cut down on the time I spent with some friends or family members because I feel happier when I am elsewhere. You will find that others are not always a good fit in your life—and that is OK. It is good that everyone doesn't have to like you, but it is even better to know that it probably isn't about you! Try the Miracle Shift Tool 1 below. Once you have done that, if the relationship continues to be painful, you may need to evaluate the relationship and also take action to protect yourself.

Making this decision to not take things personally is the most freeing thing in the world. But the law of attraction makes it imperative. If you allow yourself to stay angry or unhappy, you will attract more experiences that will make you angry or unhappy. You might try thinking that perhaps the man who cut you off in traffic just found out he owed back taxes, or his brother-in-law and six kids just moved in. Would you feel better if you thought that the clerk who is being rude possibly just lost her mother and needs your understanding and kindness? Would you enjoy your day more if you chose to think that your boss overlooked the excellent job you did because he was upset about his own performance review—and it was not because there was something unlikeable about you or your work? It is very possible that all these things are true—and how much better you might feel if you realize you have no control and decide that others' behavior is not about you!

Most behavior you find upsetting, irritating, obnoxious, or unloving is really because the other people are feeling fear, loneliness, powerlessness, and hopelessness in their own lives. Once you realize this, you can be kind and compassionate—to yourself and to them. You need to take care of yourself and make the best decisions about where you spend your time. Once you have done that, then even if a particular event or situation was awful, you can make a decision that you will not lose one more moment of happiness by taking negative people and events personally.

James Altucher, in his book *Choose Yourself*, talks about making that choice. He advises, "Only think about the people you enjoy. Only read the books you enjoy, that make you happy to be human. Only go to the events that actually make you laugh or fall in love."

Anyone Else Think This Is A Good Idea?

A thick skin is a gift from God. —Konrad Adenauer

The man who makes everything that leads to happiness depend upon himself, and not upon other men, has adopted the very best plan for living happily. —Plato

Be more concerned with your character than your reputation because your character is what you really are, while your reputation is merely what others think you are. —John Wooden

Every adversity, every failure, every heartache carries with it the seed of an equal or greater benefit. —Napoleon Hill

Adversity is the diamond dust Heaven polishes its jewels with. —Thomas Carlyle

At the end of the day, let there be no excuses, no explanation, no regrets. —Steve Maraboli

Believe in yourself and all that you are. Know that there is something inside you that is greater than any obstacle. —Christian D. Larson

My favorite:
I love criticism, just so long as it is unqualified praise. —Noel Coward

Shift for interactions with people you do not know

Decide that you will automatically assume that the actions of people you don't know well are not about you, but have to do with their own problems, difficult days, or illnesses.

- ❤ Picture yourself like water—just flow over and around any obstacles or unpleasant circumstances in your path.
- ❤ If you don't know the person's history and issues, you might try making up a scenario that would explain why he or she is being so difficult—it can make you smile and let it go.
- ❤ Decide you won't spend one more moment of your precious time trying to figure it out or blaming others or yourself.

Shift for interactions with family, friends, or those you know well

If the actions or comments are from someone you know, or are part of a family or close personal or business relationship, they will need a little more attention, since it is harder to just move on and let it go.

- ❤ First, you need to ask if there is anything for which you need ask forgiveness. If so, you will need to clear your part and apologize, even if you feel the other person has done the greater "wrong." Never expect them to reciprocate; do this for yourself. Your peace of mind will increase, even if they never reciprocate.
- ❤ Next, you can concentrate on what you do like about the person and relationship. List their positive qualities.

- ♥ Try to remember what first attracted you to this friend or partner or how a family member adds to your life.
- ♥ Do they still display those qualities? Do they do good things for you, despite their irritating or hurtful behavior?
- ♥ Now list what irritates you, and ask yourself—how important is it? If this person died tomorrow, would this comment or this behavior have mattered?
- ♥ If not, let it go—it is not worth your attention. However, if you cannot let it go, continue with the Magic Shift Tool 1.

Magic Shift Tool 1 Appreciation

There is magic in a word of praise. For one week, try ignoring what you don't like. Just give it no attention: no complaining, blaming, helpful suggestions or comments about the behavior. Direct all your attention on what others do that is lovable, admirable, and endearing. Sincerely appreciate and compliment them. Notice, appreciate and thank them for anything pleasing they do.

- ♥ If the disliked action is that of a partner, child, or family member, every day find something that deserves a compliment or a thank-you. Give extra physical affection, a hug, a touch in passing, or a pat on the shoulder.
- ♥ If the perceived offence or annoyance is that of a friend or business associate, sincerely notice this person's good qualities and mention them, particularly in the presence of others. Make an effort to find something you do like and tell this person you appreciate something he or she did and how your experience was enriched

If you keep doing this all week, I promise that things will either shift toward a better relationship, or you will clearly see that the relationship is not in your best interest.

- ♥ If the relationship is not in your best interest, you may want to consult with a trusted mentor, pastor, or counselor about the friendship or relationship and how best to protect yourself and move on with your life.
- ♥ Family relationships and blood ties do not require you to continue accepting abuse or emotional pain. You can treat the family member with kindness and courtesy and still stop or limit your contact with this person.

No matter the outcome, you can decide on forgiveness, so you can ultimately let it go and be at peace. See Shift Key 5 on letting go of the past: forgiveness and letting go is for your sake, not someone else's. And don't forget to connect to love for a few minutes every day, as it is the most important shift of all!

What Will I Get Out Of This?

Automatically assuming that anyone's apparent ill will, anger, or rejection is not about you or your ultimate worth will give you the greatest peace and freedom. In addition, that attitude of peace and inner happiness will raise your vibration and energy. That will not only draw the best out of present circumstances and relationships, but also will draw better friendships, relationships, and experiences.

- ♥ You will have more time. If it is not about you, there is no need to call anyone to discuss it—no need to mull it over or work on a better argument or the really good comeback you should have given.
- ♥ You won't be sidetracked for long by the comments or actions of others. You can pick yourself up, let the problem go, and move on without having to spend a week with your therapist or lift yourself out of anger or sadness.
- ♥ You can direct your thoughts and energies outward toward the good things you want to do in your life.

In addition, if you have done everything you can to make your closer relationships healthy and right, you will clearly see what relationships are in your best interest.

- ♥ You will know you have done your part by making right anything you may have contributed or done wrong and by treating the other party with kindness and courtesy.
- ♥ You can limit your contact with those who may be causing you continued distress or harm.

Recommended Resources You Might Enjoy

Altucher, J. (2013) *Choose Yourself,* Lioncrest Publishing
Carnegie, D (1936) *How to Win Friends and Influence People.* New York, Simon & Schuster.
Cohen, A. (2002) *Why Your Life Sucks, and What You Can Do about It.* US: Bantam.

Norwood, R. (2008) *Women Who Love Too Much: When You Keep Wishing and Hoping He'll Change.* New York: Pocket Books.

Picquette, E. (2012) *"About Your Worth" Mini Meditation – Lighten Your Heart.* MP3s available for download

Ruiz, M. (1997, 2012) *The Four Agreements: A Practical Guide to Personal Freedom.* San Rafael, Amber-Allen Publishing.

For an easy click on book list of all the reference books – go to <u>AdvisorIsIn.com</u>

Shift Key 5: Give Up On The Past

Hope inspired, The first to apologize is the bravest. The first to forgive is the strongest, and the first to forget is the happiest. Unknown

Impatience—if she existed—inspired, Learn from the past—then get the hell out of there! Unknown

or Shift 5 you will be able to retrieve your lost energy from the past. This will improve your relationships; because your past hurts can influence how you see the present. Have you ever heard anyone say, "Well, what he said wasn't that big of a deal, but if you knew about my childhood, you would understand why I felt so hurt"; or, "That's just what my father told me—I will never make anything of myself!" Holding on to the anger or sadness of the past allows the past to influence your present. Letting go was the first shift I did, and it really changed my whole outlook on life—my present and future.

The most debilitating and energy-draining activity you can do (other than worry about the future) is spending time in regret about the past. There are times—during the break-up of a significant relationship, the death or illness of a loved one, the loss of a job, or a major trauma or disability—when it is certainly appropriate to be sad or angry for a time. However, if you are thinking again and again about events from years past and decisions you made long ago, without any resolution, it is not helpful to you. In fact, fear and worry actually prevent the body from healing, according to Dr. Lissa Rankin in her book *Mind Over Medicine*.

You can shift to clear your heart of any past sadness, guilt, or resentment toward others that is lowering your vibration and attracting more of the same sad situations. You can stop wasting your precious energy.

When you complete this process you will have more lightness, playfulness, and energy to enjoy yourself and your current relationships.

I always thought I had forgiven others, but I didn't know how to let the feelings go. I would still feel sadness or regret, and I often thought about the past, hoping I would not repeat the same mistakes. My angels wanted to comfort me when I was sad or feeling regret, but since they see and know everything, they must have tried to help me see that I needed to stop. They knew that I was just recreating the vibration and emotions that would draw more people and interactions where there would be unhappiness. I was not listening—I was absorbed in feeling like a victim and wondering why such things happened to me when I was trying so hard to do my part. I believe that we are guided to the information we need most, at the time, and I certainly needed what followed: somehow I ended up reading an article that suggested that holding on to past hurts keeps people in destructive relationships and can contribute to weight issues and to illness. That got my attention! I was finally motivated to search for anything from the past that might be influencing my present situation.

When you think about unhappy events from the past, you are vibrating at that angry, sad, or regretful level in your present time, and drawing the same kind of experience into your present life. Carolyn Myss offers another way to think about regret, using an illustration like this: Visualize yourself starting out with one hundred units of energy to spend each day. If you have thirty-five units spent in anger, regret, and sadness over the past and perhaps another thirty-five units spent in worrying about the future, how much energy do you have left for enjoying today? When I thought about this, I realized that I wanted to have more than thirty units of my energy for today. I did not want my energy tied up in the past or borrowed for the future.

As far as the daily hurts we all experience—I generally like to think of myself as a forgiving and tolerant person. But I was still holding on to criticisms, slights, or comments, and I could tell by how I felt. I had a boss, at one time, who seemed to want to make my life difficult. She would ask my opinion and then disagree in front of others, and she criticized my (flawless, of course!) projects. I looked at my part and asked a colleague's opinion. I wanted to make sure that I was supportive of my boss and wasn't doing anything to cause her any discomfort. Then, because I had to work with her day after day, I chose to use the Magic Shift tool 2 (see below), and clear my resentment. I knew it had worked when I could think of her or see her in a meeting and feel neutral or positive. I no longer had that little twinge of hurt when I was around her. I was able to decide that her issues were not really about me—and my whole day was happier. Also, in response to my lightening up and changing my energy, her barbed words decreased and eventually stopped.

I found that I could tell if I have something to forgive or release by thinking about the person or event from the past. If there is a twinge of anger, resentment, or sadness, I need to release it. I have done the forgiveness exercise below several times over the last ten years, and each time I feel a new lightness of heart and an energetic shift. It is also wonderful to know that when I release the old vibrations of anger, guilt, and sadness from the past, I am less likely to attract that kind of person or situation into my present life experience.

I urge you to try the forgiveness, Magic Shift Tool 2 and 3, (below) for letting go of resentment, anger, or sadness from your past or present.

Anyone Else Think This Is A Good Idea?

Feelings are much like waves, we can't stop them from coming, but we can choose which one to surf.
—Jonathan Martensson

Sometimes life knocks you on your ass…get up, get up, get up!!! Happiness is not the absence of problems; it's the ability to deal with them. —Steve Maraboli

You can't have a better tomorrow if you are thinking about yesterday all the time. —Charles F. Kettering

Forgiveness means letting go of the past. —Gerald Jampolsky

There is only one way to happiness and that is to cease worrying about things which are beyond the power of our will.   —Epictetus

Though no one can go back and make a brand new start, anyone can start from now and make a brand new ending. —Carl Bard

Whatever does not destroy me, makes me stronger. —Nietzsche

My personal favorite:
If you don't learn from your mistakes, there's no sense making them. —Anonymous

Dare To Shift

Shift everything—releasing the past will change your life! Try the following exercises. For deeper hurts and trauma, please consider the relief offered by the Emotional Freedom Technique and other methods I have listed in the reference section. Counselors and therapists are certainly recommended; just make sure that the focus is on releasing the past and solutions for your future. Once you have been heard and understood, do not continue to identify yourself with misery, victimhood or continually repeat the feelings and story of the past hurt or sadness. If you hold on to your sadness and anger, you can think of it like a big velcro button on your chest – it will attract and hold new situations that match it. Not what you want, I am sure!

Magic Shift Tool 2 Forgiveness

Shift to forgiveness exercise: There are many versions of this—I like the image of angels, but please use what is right for you. You can choose to write out the whole exercise or just imagine saying your feelings and letting them go. Choose a time when you will be uninterrupted: Make a list of the unhappy events of your life and people who caused you anger, grief, disappointment, and sadness in your life.

- ♥ Imagine a beautiful angel appearing before you with a golden basket. See yourself gathering all your resentments, anger, grief, sadness, and the unhappy events of your life into a heap before you.
- ♥ The angel asks you to bring each individual on your list (living or dead) before you, one by one. Start your list with you. Forgive yourself for whatever you think were your mistakes or life choices that hurt you. See yourself with the angel's compassion, doing your best with what education, love and understanding that you had at the time.
- ♥ Then see each person on your list, one by one—in your imagination. Decide that you want to be free of the feelings of the past. Do this for yourself, not for them or for anyone else.
- ♥ You may know at a deep level that *you and each person* were doing the best you all could, given your and their generation, childhood, knowledge, and experiences.
- ♥ Ask the angels to give the other person the gifts (more knowledge, more love, etc.) they would have needed in order to have had a loving, happy experience, instead of what actually happened during the past event.
- ♥ Ask the angels to give you the gifts you would have needed in order to have had a loving, happy experience, instead of what happened during the past event—did you need more courage, strength, and love at that time? See yourself receiving those gifts.
- ♥ With your permission, the angels surround you with a beautiful light of love and give you courage to tell each person, seeing them before you in your imagination: "I wish that [whatever outcome you wish had happened] and I choose to release the past—I ask you to release me, and I forgive and let you go freely."
- ♥ See other angels gently escort the person away; see the person surrounded by light, and with his or her burden lighter, also.

- ♥ When you are done with your list, see the angels place all the sadness, grief, or anger that you released into the golden basket. The angels take the golden basket of sadness and anger away to be melted into compassion and peace.
- ♥ You have freed yourself from a heavy part of your past. Now, your energy and enthusiasm can go into enjoying today. You have forgiven yourself and others. You know you have done well, and you feel peaceful.

(Adapted from an exercise by Doreen Virtue and similar exercises I have developed over the years.)

Magic Shift Tool 3 Letting Go

Try this for anger and resentments that are current, or so deep you just can't let go.

There is a magical cure for resentments. This method is often used in 12-Step programs. It has made amazing changes in my life, lifting me out of despair and trauma. It is simply this:

- ♥ No matter how you feel about it, pray or ask the universe that the person for whom you feel resentment will have exactly the same kind of wonderful things, delightful relationships, health and financial success you want for yourself.
- ♥ Keep doing this daily (even if you do not want to do it) and as sincerely as you can, and you will feel a clear shift as your heart opens and lightens. You may have to say, "I don't want to do this, but I am asking for help in doing it, and I ask for the willingness to wish the very best for this person."
- ♥ What seems to make this work is that when you open your heart (even if it is hurting), the Giver of unconditional love, or angels open your eyes to see the other person as the angels do—just another fallible person doing the best they can with what they have. This moves your vibration and energy into a place where you can see your way to forgive and let them go. And don't forget to connect to love for a few minutes every day, as it is the most important shift of all!

What Will I Get Out Of This?

Freedom and a wonderful lightness of heart—most people report that they feel like a heavy burden has been lifted. If the wrong done you seems too great to let go, review the following for some additional help.

- ♥ OK, letting go of the past sounds good, but they never said they were sorry—they don't deserve it! If your thoughts are good for you, they will make you feel lighter. Do you feel lighter when you remember old wrongs? Would letting go make you feel lighter and happier? We can't change others, but we can clear our own slate, even if others never understand or ask for forgiveness. We can choose to be free!
- ♥ If I forgive them, will they change? (That might be worth it!) The forgiveness exercise will free your spirit, but don't do it to change anyone else, or to get a reaction from others. Unless you have something for which you want forgiveness, you should never mention this to the other person. Any attempt to use this forgiveness as a manipulation will backfire. The other people in your life have free choice, and they may or may not change for the better. This forgiveness exercise is for you alone.
- ♥ It is just too hard—what they did was too awful—I cannot let it go. Forgiveness does not deny responsibility for another's behavior or condone wrong—it does give you freedom to live your life. It has been wisely said that resentment is the poison you take, hoping that the other person will die. Think about it: holding onto resentment only hurts you, not them. You do not want the poison of negative energy in your life.

Recommended Resources You Might Enjoy

Bandler, Richard, (2008) *Get the Life You Want*, Florida, HCI, Inc.
Hay, L. (2009) *You Can Heal Your Life*, Hay House.
James, J., Friedman, R. (2009) *The Grief Recovery Handbook.* HarperCollins.
Picquette, E. (2012) *"About Forgiveness" Mini Meditation – Lighten Your Heart.* MP3s available for download
Rankin, L. (2013) *Mind Over Medicine, Scientific Proof That You Can Heal Yourself*, NY, Hay House
Siegel, B. (1990) *Love, Medicine and Miracles*, HarperCollins.
For an easy click on book list of all the reference books – go to AdvisorIsIn.com

I have seen the following information and methods assist many in clearing past hurts and trauma. I am listing them for your interest. If you need this help, read through the list, ask the Giver of unconditional love or your angels for help, and you will be drawn to what will work best for you.

- ♥ 12-step programs provide compassion and group support for a variety of issues, including family and survivor programs. They have been instrumental in helping millions of people find peace, no matter

the chaos and pain they are experiencing in their lives. One listing can be found at http://en.wikipedia.org/wiki/List_of_twelve-step_groups
- Emotional Freedom Technique—EFT. EFT uses a simple tapping sequence on various meridian points while feeling and describing the traumatic feelings as a way for the body or cellular memory to release the traumatic event or feelings. More information can be found at http://www.EFTuniverse.com Also, Robert Smith, of Healing Magic, provides many excellent educational videos using Faster EFT on YouTube. http://youtu.be/hGZ1VuJ21Uk

Shift Key 6: Expect The Best Future

Hope inspired, *Good morning. This is God. I will be handling all of your problems today. I will not need your help, so have a miraculous day.* —Wayne Dyer

Impatience—if she existed—inspired, *Be careful about reading health books. You may die of a misprint.* —Mark Twain

or the sixth Shift Key, you can retrieve all your energy wasted in useless worry about the future and look forward with hope. How much more fun could you have if you were hopeful about the future? How much energy are you losing when you worry about uncontrollable things that may happen someday? I would say, a lot! How much fun is it to be in relationship with someone who is anxious or worried? In addition, when you are in the low energy of anxiety and worry, you are actually attracting the very people and things about which you are worried. Unless you are actively coming up with a plan to make the problem less likely to happen, it is just wasted energy. The angels want you to use this wasted energy to dream up and carry out great ways to enjoy yourself and your relationships.

The angels of inspiration are always with you to help you move on from worry. As a child, I thought that the angels and universe would prevent all harm. When I realized that bad things still happened, I lost some of my feeling of security and safety. Later, I learned the following:

- ❤ I live in a world of contrast: light and darkness. If I didn't see what seems dark, I could not appreciate or choose the light.

- ♥ I have free choice, and the angels and universe do not interfere unless I ask, and even then they do not always interfere with the consequences of my choices.
- ♥ I would like to grow through joy, and the angels want me to as well. But I don't seem to listen or be willing to see my part in my problems unless I suffer what I think is a setback. Only then am I more open to see myself and choose a better way.
- ♥ The love of the angels, the Giver of love and life, or the force that holds the stars in place is always available for me. No matter what happens, I can trust that I will be supported and loved through the experience.

I liked the thought that I would be helped and loved, no matter what, and I have found that to be true in each dark experience in my life. But after all the work I had done in understanding the law of attraction, I wanted to do everything in my power to have less of those unhappy experiences. If my energy and vibration of worry, anxiety, and fear would attract things that matched worry, anxiety, and fear, then I wanted to let my worry go. I wanted to attract more positive things, people, and events in my life. I found that it helped if I could break down my fears and anxieties into two parts: global anxiety and personal anxiety.

Global Anxiety

This anxiety is usually about epidemics, crime, war, and the economy. The media is generally filled with global anxiety: bad news about crime, the economy, and the state of the world. Listen to the news, and it is hard to remain positive about life. The news concentrates on fear and dread—unfortunately that seems to be what attracts the largest audience. Most of the global concerns you will see revolve around safety and economics. You may find it helps to put the news into perspective if you remember the following:

- ♥ Safety—the news shows the 1 percent of the world having tragedy, all day, and over and over; while you hear nothing about the 99 percent of the world who had a good day. Ask yourself how often do the global tragedies you worry about actually happen to you? Will your worry make any difference? Most of your fears never, ever happen; yet you may spend your "good times" in fear and dread of nothing. You can choose to send aid to others, when you can. And you can then choose to ignore the bad news and be grateful and happy about the good things in your own life.
- ♥ The economy—if you think about it, you know that in the worst of times, many people thrive, and in the very best of times some people go bankrupt. During the Great Depression, some of the greatest

fortunes were built. With every economic downturn, new opportunities are born. So you can choose to look for the opportunities and take action on what you can, or you can go into a paralysis of fear. Try watching the news with the above perspective—the negative reports will recede into the background of your life, along with everything else that you really can't control. You also might try skipping the news, if you can. The people around you will let you know if anything important happens!

Personal Anxiety And Worry

This is most often about relationships and money, or the lack of either. Set aside some time to get a good grasp on everything about which you spend time worrying.

- ❤ What are the issues that you worry about the most? Write them down.
- ❤ Which of your worries are completely beyond your control? Cross those out—see global anxiety, above.

For worries that you can do something about, make a plan to take whatever action you can. Once you have taken reasonable action, then let the rest become part of the worries beyond your control.

Anyone Else Think This Is A Good Idea?

Keep your heart free from hate, your mind from worry. —Norman Vincent Peale

Once a decision was made, I didn't worry about it afterward. —Harry S. Truman

I'm not afraid of storms, for I'm learning to sail my ship. —Louisa May Alcott

Most of us have far more courage than we ever dreamed we possessed. —Dale Carnegie

Anxiety does not empty tomorrow of its sorrow, but only empties today of its strength. —Charles Spurgeon.

Whatever you're thinking about is literally like planning a future event. When you're worrying, you are planning, when you're appreciating, you are planning….
What are you planning? —Abraham-Hicks

And my favorite:
Today is the tomorrow we worried about yesterday. —Unknown

Global and personal worries

Shift to let go of what you can never control. The answer for both global worries and for personal worries that are out of your control is the same.

- ♥ Recognize your utter lack of power to make a difference. Logically—why waste your time?
- ♥ Recognize that most things you have worried about in the past never, ever happened.
- ♥ Ask your angels of inspiration and the Giver of all that is to help you let go of what you can never control.
- ♥ Try EFT —see sources listed below for help in releasing deep fears and anxieties.
- ♥ Once you have let go of some your worry, try the "Heart Blessing" audio MP3 listed below, and ask the angels and universe to bring you all the positive and beautiful things you want for yourself and your family. Try it—it will give you a positive perspective about your day and your life.

Surely the power that keeps the earth spinning can handle global problems far better than you can, so let it go. You can do nothing about any of them, so connect to love. Spend some time breathing deeply and relaxing, and ask the angels to take the fears away, or picture yourself just handing over what you can't control to the power that keeps the stars in place.

Your job or your health

Shift to take action, if there is something you can do. When there is something you can do that will help, do what you can, then relax, knowing you have done your best.

- ♥ Is this something that is totally out of your control such as an fear of an accident or job cutbacks? See solution for global anxiety.
- ♥ Is this is something about which you can do some preparation or prevention? If so, make a list of actions and schedule time to do what you can, then relax. An example of this might be developing a plan for how your family could contact each other if the phones were down, or setting up bank accounts to start an emergency savings fund.
- ♥ If you are still worried, ask yourself - What is the worst possible thing that could happen?

- If that "worst possible thing" actually happened, what would you do?
- Face that worst possible fear and make a plan. Decide what you would do, if this fear ever became real. For example, if you lost your job, what would you do? Having a plan and knowing how much savings you have, how much you actually need to live each month and with whom you would network may help. Taking the actions you can take to handle the worst possible thing can stop your fear and allow you to feel more peace.

Unfulfilling or missing relationships

You attract friends or lovers at the same vibration and energy level you are at. So if you are lonely and depressed or unexcited about life, your present partner or whomever you attract will likely be someone who is also feeling depressed and lost. Great books have been written about this subject; see the list of further readings below. But here are some practical tools to open your heart and begin to shift present relationships or the relationships you attract:

- The secret is to change *you*. Start becoming the type of person you want to be with: loyal, warm, kind, successful in whatever they do, attractively dressed, and well mannered.
- What have you wanted to do, but have been waiting to do? Would you like to travel, dance, go back to school, learn a language, or volunteer?
- Stop waiting for your partner to change or to find a partner. Get busy and start living your life now!
- Treat your life as if you only had a year to live—what would you do in that year?
- When you are busy and having fun with your own life, then someone with an equal energy and love for life will appear: either your current partner will change to match you, or they will drift out of your life, someone new will appear—looking for someone just like you!

Money—there is never enough

This also is a large subject, and there are many books and classes about getting out of debt, understanding the energy of money, and finding work you love. (See the list of further readings below.) But while you search out the sources that can help you with your particular money issues—here are some things that will immediately begin to shift your money attraction.

- ♥ Take a moment whenever you receive any money—paycheck, gift, or other—and give thanks for the money that has come to you. You will get more of what you decide to appreciate.
- ♥ When you pay your bills or shop—switch your thinking. Shift from—"They should not charge so much, I can't afford this!" Instead—think to yourself—"Thank you" for the electricity, the air conditioning, the water, and a car to drive; for the beautiful clothing, as you pay each bill or as you shop.
- ♥ Make a gratitude list every night before you sleep. This is a small thing that can change your attitude and your life. Go to sleep appreciating what you do have, and expecting more.
- ♥ Examine your beliefs about wealth. Do you believe it is virtuous or good to be poor? Recognize that money is just a tool, and, like everything else, it can be used for good or ill. Wealth or poverty does not determine character or good choices. Money is neither good nor bad. Good people need money to do good things.
- ♥ Abraham-Hicks in the book, *Money and the Law of Attraction*, suggests always carrying $100 or more in your wallet. Hold your money and appreciate it (you don't need to spend it). Just note everything you could buy, all day—if you really wanted to buy! Notice how good it is to have money. Stay positive about how good you will feel when you have even more.
- ♥ Give yourself $1000 of pretend money in a notebook, and double it every day. Every day pretend to spend the money on whatever you would like to do or have. Write down what you are pretend-buying and the price, using up all the money each day. Visualize how good or fun it will be to have the item. Understand that money is just a tool or energy to get what you want.

There is no lack in the universe. There is no lack of health, good friends, or money. As Abraham-Hicks notes, it has not been that long since we were trading chickens and furs for our needs. Where did all that money come from?

If you do these exercises, your heart will open, and your energy will change from lack to appreciation. Your expectations and energy control your health, the people and relationships you attract, and the money you receive. Switch to gratitude. Appreciate what you have, expect what is good and choose to enjoy everything you have *now*. And don't forget to connect to love for a few minutes every day, as it is the most important shift of all!

What Will I Get Out Of This?

An extra two hours per day!

A British writer for the Daily Mail in 2011 estimated that many Britons fret more than 2.5 hours per day, and they are likely not alone. If that seems excessive, think about the time you think while driving, in the bathroom, and in the shower. Are you thinking positive thoughts of gratitude? Probably not…. At least, I don't always think thoughts of gratitude! Perhaps you can allow yourself a few minutes of fretting and planning on productive subjects, where some planning or action may change the outcome and make you feel more secure. If you stopped worrying about the potential global disasters and things totally beyond your control, that would free up possibly two hours a day. Dr. Siegel cited a study that got my attention – Patients in a control group for a new chemotherapy drug were given nothing but saline, yet they were warned it could be chemotherapy and 30% of them lost their hair. Do not underestimate the power of your thoughts! You could be thinking about something positive, uplifting, or fun with your time. Worrying and fretting fall way down the emotional and vibrational scale, somewhere between despair and frustration. Remember—shifting to peace and gratitude will raise your vibration and attract more for which to be grateful.

Recommended Resources You Might Enjoy

Attwood, J. (2008) *The Passion Test: The Effortless Path to Discovering Your Life Purpose*. New York, Penguin Group.
Carnegie, D. (1944*)* *How to Stop Worrying and Start Living*. New York: Simon and Schuster.
Ford, A. (2011) *The Soulmate Secret: Manifest the Love of Your Life with the Law of Attraction*. New York, Harper Collins
Nemeth, M. (2000) *The Energy of Money: A Spiritual Guide to Financial and Personal Fulfillment*. New York, Random House.
Picquette, E. (2012) "About Worry" on *Mini Meditation —Lighten Your Heart* MP3 available for download
Siegel, B. (1990) *Love, Medicine and Miracles*, NY, HarperCollins.
Ramsey, D. (2009) *The Total Money Makeover: A Proven Plan for Financial Fitness*. Nashville: Thomas Nelson, Inc.
For an easy click on book list of all the reference books – go to AdvisorIsIn.com

Shift Key 7: Appreciate Everything Now

Hope inspired, *Imagine what would happen, if we all woke up today with only the things and people we gave love and thanks to yesterday?* —Will Rivera

Impatience—if she existed—inspired, *As a child, my family's menu consisted of two choices: take it or leave it.* —Buddy Hackett

ow, you actually have time for Shift 7! You have the time and attention to enjoy the present moment. Once you have stopped mulling over and regretting the past and have cut down on needless fretting and worry over the future, you can savor the present. How much more fun could you have and how much more could you enjoy your partner, friends, and family if you are really appreciating the present moment? Have you ever wondered why you get your best ideas while in the shower? Have you wondered why you sometimes feel closest to your partner when you are walking on the beach? Have you wondered why you are happier and more energetic when you take a walk in nature? In those settings you are more relaxed: your mind is quieter, and your heart is more open to appreciating the present and to the energy of angels, the universe, or inspiration. You can learn to live in and appreciate the present, in any setting, just about all the time, if you want.

Possibly I lived in the present and appreciated more when I was a child. I hope so. However, from the time I was a teenager, until the last ten years, I very seldom really enjoyed the present. I was physically standing in the present, but my mind was reliving my past mistakes or jumping into the future and my to-do list and how I could improve. I just wasn't aware there was another way to live. I had read about staying in the present, but after years of practice living in the past and the future, I didn't even know what that meant. I had to clear out and forgive the past and give up the fearful future, in order to even get a glimpse of what it was to be present and enjoy the little pleasures and delights all around me.

As I released and forgave my past and gave my worries about the future to the universe and my angels, I discovered what it was like to "be here now." For example, I remember going to a beautiful lake most weekends in my thirties. It took me two or three hours before I could let go of my worries and plans enough to relax and even notice the beautiful scenery and water around me. Even more important, I know I was not fully present during my daughter's early years. I did all the mothering actions to the best of my ability, but my mind was usually elsewhere. I am sure that I missed a lot of love, fun, and enjoyment while I was thinking about the past or making mental lists about tomorrow. My daughter still likes to go out to eat with me more than for me to cook at home. I know that is because at home, I am always thinking about the food I am preparing, how to clean up, or something else that needs to be done—just about anything other than spending time and attention on her. When we go out, I can really listen and put my attention on her and on our experience together.

I am much better at being in the present today. By doing forgiveness work for the past and learning to trust the future, I have cleared most of my past regrets and future worries—and changed my experience of life. A couple of years ago, I was driving to Lake Havasu. I had my favorite music on and was singing in the car—I was happy and totally in the present moment, enjoying the scenery and the music. After a while, I happened to look in my rearview mirror and noticed that a police car was following me with lights flashing. With the music cranked up, I had not heard the siren. I pulled over, knowing I probably hadn't slowed down sufficiently while driving through the speed zone in the last little town.

I had a moment of anxiety. I even mentally said to my angels, "What happened to the law of attraction—I was so happy!" Then I decided that whatever happens, this will not ruin my day. I would just take care of this, and my wonderful weekend was still ahead. Turns out the policeman had been following me for a while. He was polite when he asked me if I knew he had had his lights and siren on for a few miles—but he obviously went back to his car to write my ticket. I just sat and breathed deeply and let it go—it was out of my control at the moment, and I knew it was really OK if I got a ticket. A minute or two later he came back and said, "You are one lucky lady! I just got another emergency call. Promise me you will slow down, and I will let you go. Have a good weekend!"

Now, I was delighted with being let off with a warning. But there was a much bigger awareness for me. I was different—I was fine with getting a ticket. I would have had a great day and a great weekend, no matter what. Years before, I would have felt embarrassment and anxiety for not paying attention to the speed trap. Whether I got a ticket or not, I would have worried about my inattention and the implications of getting a ticket for the rest of the weekend. Now, with my new mind-set, I knew I could be happy no matter what happened. The ticket would not have changed anything really important in my life. I was enjoying my day and appreciating my surroundings so much that it would take a lot to change my happiness. I was living the day in gratitude, and finally I was really in the present.

Anyone Else Think This Is A Good Idea?

With the past, I have nothing to do; nor with the future. I live now. —Ralph Waldo Emerson

If the only prayer you said was thank you, that would be enough. —Meister Eckhart

Enjoy the little things, for one day you may look back and realize they were the big things. —Robert Brault

If you want to turn your life around, try thankfulness. It will change your life mightily. —Gerald Good

In daily life we must see that it is not happiness that makes us grateful, but gratefulness that makes us happy. —Brother David Steindl-Rast

Gratitude is absolutely the way to bring more into your life. —Marci Shimoff

Feeling gratitude and not expressing it is like wrapping a present and not giving it. —William Arthur Ward

And my favorite:
Walk as if you are kissing the Earth with your feet. —Thich Nhat Hanh

Dare To Shift

Shift part one: Shift your thoughts to gratitude and appreciation.

- ♥ Depending on whether you are a morning or evening person, find two or three minutes daily and record a gratitude list of at least five things each day. You can put it in your notes in your phone, or computer, or in a bedside journal. Another way is to spend your last few minutes each night before sleep thanking the Giver of love and life and your angels for things you appreciate. It is a great way to go to sleep with a peaceful, open heart.
- ♥ Once you are looking for things for which to be grateful, you will start to see more and more to appreciate. When you appreciate something, you are telling the universe that you want more of it. This will change your life in wonderful ways, but you must do the work—spend the few minutes on your list each day.
- ♥ One you start noticing all the nice things that show up, mentally say thank you whenever you see something that pleases you. One of my friends always thanks the parking angels when she gets a good parking space. I like to sit, enjoy a wonderful meal, and just be thankful for each delicious bite, then I look around at my friends, and I can usually say, "There is no where else I would rather be—thank you!" What matters is your attitude of appreciation for each gift and pleasure in life.

Shift part two: Look for and expect silver linings in your clouds:

If some annoyance or unhappy event happens, think of how it might be a good thing. If it is a major disappointment, even though you may not be able to see it now, perhaps something better may result. The following are some examples:

- ♥ If you miss a turn, you may have missed road construction.
- ♥ If you are stuck behind a slow driver in traffic, perhaps you are missing an accident up ahead.
- ♥ If you are late, maybe there is a good reason. I often find that when I just let my worry go and ask the universe to get me where I need to be at just the right time, either the other person is also late, somehow I arrive on time, or the appointment has to be changed anyway.
- ♥ Rejection may be protection—I once didn't get a hospital attorney position that I thought I really wanted. I was very disappointed—and at that time, I felt that my angels and the universe had obviously made a big mistake. It turned out that the hospital closed within six months. In retrospect, I was really glad that I did not get the job I thought I wanted.

Shift part three: Be present—if your mind wanders away from what your partner or child is saying or from your current activity, ask yourself if what you are thinking about is really more important than the person you are with. If not, return your attention to enjoying what you are actually doing right now. Enjoy the people in your life right now. Take the time to really listen to your children and your partner, right now. Look at each event that happens with an open heart—suspend your judgment and look at what you are doing or observing with curiosity, openness, and acceptance. Some possibilities include the following:

- Walk outdoors, and pretend you must describe everything to someone who cannot see, smell, taste, or touch. Look at the scenery and sky; notice the temperature and the dryness or humidity of the air. Touch a leaf or flower, noticing their textures and colors. Breathe in slowly, and notice any particular scents in the air.
- Be with your child or partner, and just savor everything—notice their expressions, what they are interested in—without judging, criticizing, instructing, or having any other agenda. If they are open to it, share a hug and breathe in their scent, their feel, and their wonderful sweetness. If it is appropriate, tell them how much they mean to you.
- Find something good to eat and stop and think how you would describe it to someone who had never had it. (Note: chocolate might work well.) Savor the color, taste, texture, and aroma—slow down, put down your fork or the food between bites, and enjoy each bite.

Last, should you find yourself straying into anything negative from the past or the future, ask yourself if what you are mulling over will be important in one year. If it won't be important, you can think about it later. Don't waste another precious moment on it—savor your present. And don't forget to connect to love for a few minutes every day, as it is the most important shift of all!

What Will I Get Out Of This?

The more you open your heart to appreciate, the more you will find in your world to appreciate. Dr. Seligman, in his book *Authentic Happiness* conducted studies showing that depressed patients, who daily listed three good things that happened to them in an on-line journal, reported feeling better within 15 days. When you bask in the good times and savor each moment, the universe and the law of attraction will bring even better moments and experiences. This is the way to a life of more abundance and greater enjoyment. There are three parts to this, and you have a start.

- ♥ Past—Gratitude for the good things you have received and gratitude for the worrisome things that did not happen.
- ♥ Present—Appreciation for all the beautiful people and events around you as you move through your day. You will start to recognize them more as you practice putting them on your gratitude list.
- ♥ Future—Expecting to appreciate and be grateful. You will begin to expect good things to come, and know that even if something does not appear to be what you wanted, it may turn out to be for the best.

When you learn to expect that, no matter what it looks like, life is working out for you—your life is so much more relaxed!

You will learn that even disappointments and rejection can turn out for the best, lessening their sting. If you try to look for the best and appreciate every situation, you will experience the truth of a popular saying: sometimes rejection is protection or redirection. This is true of events and relationships. If an event, person, or relationship is for you, the universe won't capriciously let you miss it. You will know that it is right. The other person will know that it is right, too. There will be no struggle. You will have to work to reject it. If you are rejected for a job or a relationship, you can know that it was not for you, right now. You can look at disappointment in a different way. You can see clearly that you do not know the future and the best answers for you. So you can do what you can, then let go and just enjoy and savor the present. You can know and expect that the best will work out. This is part of the path to a peaceful state of mind and a lot more happiness.

Recommended Resources You Might Enjoy

Hay, L. et al. (2004) *Gratitude: A Way of Life*, US: Hay House.
Hicks, E. (2006) *The Law of Attraction,* US: Hay House.
Picquette, E. (2012) "Connecting to Love" and "Heart Blessings" on *Mini Meditation—Shift Keys*, MP3 available for download
Ryan, M. J. (1999) *Attitudes of Gratitude: How to Give and Receive Joy Every Day of Your Life*, NY: Conari Press.
Seligman, M. (2004) *Authentic Happiness*, NY, Simon & Schuster
Shimoff, M. (2009) *Happy for No Reason: 7 Steps for Being Happy from the Inside Out*. New York, Simon & Schuster.
For an easy click on book list of all the reference books – go to AdvisorIsIn.com

♥ ♥ ♥

Shift Key 8: Re-Choose Your Relationships

Hope inspired, We are each of us angels with only one wing, and we can only fly by embracing one another. —Luciano de Crescenzo

Impatience—if she existed—inspired, Just like a shoe, if someone is meant for you, they will fit just perfectly. No forcing, no struggling and no pain. —Unknown

In Shift Key 8, you will move your focus further outward. It is time to look at your relationships and know that you have a choice with whom you spend your precious time and life. If you have tried the preceding shifts, my wish is that you are finding it easier to appreciate yourself and the wonderful things in your life. Happy, satisfying relationships are one of the greatest indicators of a happy life. You might think of life as a journey—a long bus or train trip. People get off and on, but the people sitting closest to you can greatly enhance or damage your experience on the journey. Now that you are living more in the present, with less worry and more appreciation, it is time to look around at your relationships. With whom are you spending your life, and are those relationships happy and supportive?

    I had always known that I deserved supportive relationships that built me up and helped me to be the best I could be. Yet I often stayed in unrewarding friendships and relationships because I was afraid of being alone, or I was afraid of not being good enough if I reached out for something new. As I look back, I can see times when I was at a fork in my path. My angels were tapping me on the shoulder and telling me to go toward what made me feel light and happy. But because of my lack of confidence in myself, I often took the hard way—I often held on to people, jobs, and relationships that did not work for me. I thought I had no choice, and I had to make unworkable relationships work. I had the misguided idea that if I would be more lovable or likeable, I could make other people like or love me. Of course staying in unhappy situations didn't help me feel good about myself. I didn't realize that I had to like and love myself, first. I was still stuck in the belief that others should change, not realizing that they would never change because of my wishes or efforts. I eventually learned that if I could love myself, I would treat myself better and be able to choose friends and romantic relationships that supported me rather than caused pain.

But that took me awhile—I didn't realize I was making poor choices in relationships. I thought that if I just read more books and learned better techniques for communicating, then surely my relationships would improve and others would change. I was partially right. I did learn a lot, and nothing we learn is ever lost. However, I was still trying to be good enough, rather than appreciating my unique goodness. During this time I had a couple of wonderful experiences in learning to love myself. I was in a relationship where the man I was dating was very attentive and fun and then would just disappear. If I accepted that he was gone and started to live my own life, then he would come back and do something nice to keep me in the relationship. As part of my job at the time, I was attending a group for people in treatment for addictions and abusive relationships. I thought I was the healthy one in the group. I will never forget the feeling I had when I was sharing about this relationship and the whole group shook their heads in disbelief. Didn't I get it that he was not going to change? It is funny in retrospect, but until that moment, I still had hopes that I could change something and someone totally out of my control.

Another time, I was struggling to make a difficult relationship work, and, while I was meditating and opening my heart to ask for help, I heard a voice in my heart say clearly, "He does not wish you well." I believe the voice was my angels', and I am grateful. I took their advice and was able to make a choice that honored me. My angels were telling me all along that I was lovable, as I was. I had just chosen the wrong relationships, because I didn't believe I was lovable.

That was my experience, and I am sure yours is different, but take a moment now and review your three to five closest relationships. What kinds of friends, family, and romantic relationships are in your life right now? Dr Rankin, in *Mind Over Medicine* cites numerous studies indicating that relationships affect your health more than what you eat or how you exercise. Here is a list of some of the qualities that I use to evaluate what kind of friend and partner I am and the standard for what I expect from my friends. You can make your own list.

I want to *be* this kind of friend or partner and have this kind of friend and partner—someone who is

- ♥ kind—they build you up rather than tear you down;
- ♥ trustworthy—they do what they say they will do and speak the truth;
- ♥ open and fun—they are willing to try new activities and pastimes;
- ♥ optimistic—they expect to have a good experience and that things will turn out well;
- ♥ reciprocal—they share and give to others as often as they take; and
- ♥ loyal—they have your best interests at heart.

Once you have made your own list, then choose to be this kind of friend and seek this kind of friend or partner.

Here is another, more general way to evaluate the friendships in your life. There is a wonderful quote from Jack Canfield of the *Chicken Soup* series. "Look at the five people you spend the most time with. Add up all their incomes and divide it by five. That's about how much you're making right now." I believe that who we spend the most time with also influences all areas of our lives, not just money. Think about the five people or couples you spend the most time with—what are they like and how are they influencing you in the following areas?

- ♥ How much money and success you have
- ♥ How positive you are, and how much you appreciate your family and your life
- ♥ How much fitness and health you have
- ♥ How much you contribute to your community

You probably would really like to be a person who can influence others to the good. However, in a group of friends or associates, it is much more likely that you will be brought down or up to the average of the group. If you are not where you want to be in your life regarding money, relationships, or health, I suggest that you take a look at where you are spending your time. Take a look at the five people, couples, or families you spend the most time with—do they have what you want? If not, you may want to broaden your group of friends and associates. Seek out groups to join where there are people who are successfully living the values and the life path that you want for yourself. Where can you go to be inspired to be the kind of person you want to be?

If you find that you have any painful and unfulfilling relationships, you may need to make some choices. As you make choices, you know you always want to go toward love, not away from fear. However, sometimes this can be confusing:

- ♥ You may think that you must stay in a difficult situation or relationship to show love to someone else.
- ♥ You may think that you must be brave and tolerate abuse because you are invested in a marriage, or so you have money to protect your children.
- ♥ You may still be hoping that your friend, partner, or boss will change.

But you must understand that some people simply are not reciprocal. They are incapable of giving back, no matter what you do. Because of their own choices, they are interested only in their views and their desires. You could give to them and share with them forever, and they would not be concerned with your issues. Only you can determine if that is true in your situation. If you are sacrificing yourself for your children, your boss, or someone else, remember that you cannot really help or care for others, unless you first meet your own needs and take care of yourself.

Anyone Else Think This Is A Good Idea?

Surround yourself with positive people. Find people who will challenge you, believe in you and inspire you to improve. —Vicki Hitzges

Be courteous to all, but intimate with few, and let those few be well tried before you give them your confidence. —George Washington

Lots of people want to ride with you in the limo, but what you want is someone who will take the bus with you when the limo breaks down. —Oprah Winfrey

The sincere friends of this world are as ship lights in the stormiest of nights. —Giotto di Bondone

Think where man's glory most begins and ends, and say my glory was, I had such friends. —William Butler Yeats

A successful marriage requires falling in love many times, always with the same person. —Mignon McLaughlin

All marriages are happy. It's the living together afterward that causes all the trouble. —Raymond Hull

My favorite:
The best time to make friends is before you need them. —Ethel Barrymore

Dare To Shift

Shift for imperfect relationships.

If your relationship or friendship has value, but just needs some improvement—try this:

- ♥ Visualize what you want in a friend or lover—in detail. Imagine how you would feel if you were in loving relationships like that. Spend a little time each day feeling that you deserve the good, and how it would feel to be in the great relationships you want. (Make sure you are imagining the good you want, staying in the positive feelings—if you are just lamenting over what you lack in your relationship, you will only get more lack.)

- ♥ Just ignore what is negative, for now. Nothing you have said or done, so far, has made any change. Anger, whining, or complaining never works, anyway.
- ♥ Maintain the mind-set that you deserve this kind of wonderful relationship or friendship, as you stay positive and move on with enjoying your life, no matter what the other person does. Instead of critiquing this person, turn your attention toward yourself. Go over your list and really try to be the kind of partner you would want.
- ♥ Express sincere appreciation to your friend or partner for the good parts of the relationship. Be generous with physical affection, if appropriate, continuing to ignore anything irritating or negative.
- ♥ When you do this, you stop fighting what the relationship looks like right now. Once you stop fighting and trying to force change, you give the angels a chance to arrange the better outcome that you have requested.
- ♥ If you do this, your current relationships will either change into more of what you dreamed, or they will drift out of your life (and that will be OK)! New, happier, and more-positive relationships will materialize.

Shift for unhappy or abusive relationships.

If you have tried the above shift, and you still feel that you are in a relationship or friendship that is abusive or tears you down, you may need to make a hard choice. Remember, you are an infinite being, totally worthy of being loved and respected, and you always have a choice!

- ♥ Move toward loving you and the beautiful being that you are!
- ♥ Move toward people and groups that have a positive, uplifting purpose. You will find more positive people in groups that stand for something, rather than against.
- ♥ Know that you deserve to share your heart with someone who will respond lovingly.

So if you are in a difficult relationship with a partner, friend, family member, or coworker, talk with a trusted counselor or pastor for help. Ask yourself what you would do right now, if you really loved yourself. Look at your relationships and ask, "Have I chosen a safe person and place to open my heart?" Then, with help, re-choose your relationships. And don't forget to connect to love for a few minutes every day, as it is the most important shift of all!

What Will I Get Out Of This?

If you move toward making great choices in friends and relationships, their positive influence will enhance and inspire your life. Each time you move toward people you admire or join an inspiring group, you will be uplifted. When you move away from unhappy or critical groups or relationships, you will feel relief and lightness. Some groups you might want to try include the following:

- ♥ Rotary International and others like it—I found these organizations to be full of successful men and women who want to enjoy their fellowship and give back to their communities.
- ♥ Andrew Carnegie Courses can help overcome shyness and self-doubt in a supportive positive atmosphere.
- ♥ Toastmasters is excellent for those who want to learn to be comfortable in front of groups
- ♥ 12-Step Programs—if you need help—either in dealing with a problem area or if you have family members with addictions—these groups are unmatched.
- ♥ Churches, synagogues, and temples—many wonderful groups and support can be found in church organizations—if that fits in your life.

One rule as you try out new friends and new groups—you may feel out of place or that no one recognizes you or welcomes you. You may want to give up and decide it just wasn't for you. Don't. If you find that the group appeals to you or has value, commit to going to the group for seven times before you give up. That is approximately how much time it takes for most of people to begin to feel part of a group. Don't give up before then. Ask the angels of unconditional love to give you a hint: Where can you go to be with admirable people and be inspired to be the kind of person you want to be? Who do you want sitting next to you on your life's journey?

Recommended Resources You Might Enjoy

Carnegie, D. (1936) *How to Win Friends and Influence People,* NY: Simon and Schuster.
Carnegie Training (2011) *Make Yourself Unforgettable,* New York: Simon & Schuster.
Glass, L. (1998) *Attracting Terrific People: How to Find—and Keep—the People Who Bring Your Life Joy,* New York: St. Martin Press.

Picquette, E. (2012) "About Friendship and Romance," on *Mini Meditation—Lighten Your Heart*—MP3 available for download.

Rankin, L. (2013) *Mind Over Medicine, Scientific Proof That You Can Heal Yourself*, NY, Hay House

Thomas, M. (2004) *Personal Village: How to have people in your life by choice, not chance*, Seattle: Milestone Books.

For an easy click on book list of all the reference books – go to AdvisorIsIn.com

Shift Key 9: Handle Conflict With Grace

Hope inspired, How wonderful it must be to speak the language of the angels, with no words for hate and a million words for love! —Eileen Elias Freeman

Impatience—if she existed—inspired, A happy home is one in which each spouse grants the possibility that the other may be right, though neither believes it. —Don Fraser

hift Key 9 covers a double-sided topic. You will find communication ideas to help you gently get what you need as well as a plan for dealing with unkind remarks from others. You can use these methods to avoid or minimize conflicts that could keep your relationships unhappy for days. Sometimes in life you have to communicate on difficult subjects to present your own needs and resolve conflicts. On the other hand, you have to learn how to handle the suggestions of others that may seem like criticism and attack. These are the times when you will need to open your heart to the grace of the angels. When you can take the high road and stay in a high-energy openhearted place, you will draw the best out of the people around you. You will have more good times, and life will be so much better.

In my early career and relationships, I didn't know how to ask for what I wanted in a positive way. Initially, I just hoped that someone would read my mind. When that didn't happen, then I complained and felt mistreated. That didn't work any better. I needed to learn how to communicate with an open heart. I wanted to have my needs met without using critical language or attitude. I discovered ways to filter out whether what I wanted to say was really going to be helpful. Even if I felt my criticism or complaints were justified, what I really wanted most were good relationships. I had to start considering how I could get what I needed without damaging myself or anyone else. So here are some ideas that helped me learn to say what I wanted, while protecting my relationships.

First—I wanted to know how to communicate my desires from my heart, in the most positive way. I learned that the heart speaks best in feelings. My wishes and wants were understood best when I stayed in my feelings. Others find it harder to argue with feelings and easier to empathize or understand. I also learned that when I was communicating with anyone about what I wanted, I had to stop first and consider what I ultimately really wanted: a happy relationship. I have learned to pause before I talk about anything that might have emotional impact. Then I consider the following:

- ❤ Is this the best time to talk about this? Is the other person in the middle of something? Do we both need to eat or rest first?
- ❤ Is this something I really need, or need to discuss? Will this be important a year from now? Five years from now? Can I just let it go and do what I need to be happy myself? This weeds out 98% of any of my issues!
- ❤ Will what I am about to say bring us closer? Is there another solution that could meet everyone's needs? A solution that would not make anyone wrong?
- ❤ If it won't bring us closer, is it really absolutely necessary (necessary for my happiness—not for their improvement, education, or because they deserve to hear how upset I am)?
- ❤ If it is necessary, can I limit it to a feeling statement—what I want and why I *feel* I need it (how getting or not getting it makes me feel)?
- ❤ Can I make sure I do not criticize, accuse, or (most important) bring up the past?

Try these questions to help you filter out your most damaging comments and remind you to make sure your comments are really necessary, kind, and will bring you closer.

Second—I wanted to learn how to react from my heart, when I was criticized, verbally attacked, or caught in an argument. I didn't know what to do or how to respond to criticism, other than being utterly crushed and defensive. Attack or criticism often comes unexpectedly. So I found it was really helpful to have a plan for what I would do if it happened. After years of handling patient complaints and unhappy people in my risk-management career, I learned to use the same techniques in my personal life. I found the following plan helpful. Try this—it may go against everything you want to do—but holding your tongue and using restraint will pay off:

- ♥ Don't argue or attack in return—argument never works! Just listen. Ask if the person you're talking to has any more to say. Let him or her just run down. Your first impulse may be to react by either attacking or criticizing the speaker—but that will only invite more negative behavior.
- ♥ Don't try to explain your side and defend yourself—that is like telling the other person they are wrong, and they will likely just try to prove their point over again.
- ♥ See if you can find something you can agree upon. This is very important—the verbal attacker or criticizer really wants to be heard or wants let off steam.
- ♥ If there is something you can agree on, it shows you heard the speaker and creates common ground. This will also stop any verbal fight or argument.
- ♥ When you agree with them, there is nothing to argue about (examples: "I agree the lines are long and it is difficult to wait"; "You have a point about Jimmy's schoolwork"; "If that happened to me I would be upset, too"; "I can understand why my coming home late upset you"; "I can understand why that made you angry"; "You could be right about that"; "I hear you, and I am sure we can work this out"; "I hear what you said; let me think about it for a few minutes").
- ♥ Always acknowledge that you have heard their message. If they want to talk further, state that you will get back to them later.
- ♥ Then leave the room or the area, if you can—this gives you time to think, connect to love, and ask for insight and support.

One way the angels helped me to look at this type of interchange is by asking - *How can I handle this in a way that leaves both me and the other person whole and unhurt?* One of the best illustrations for handling criticism or argument is the phrase "Stay in the 'I' of the hurricane." Being attacked and criticized can feel like you have entered a terrible storm of feelings—anger, hurt, disbelief. There is always a calm center in a hurricane. The storm can be all around you, but you can stay in the center and act peacefully and with purpose.

Once the interaction has ended, there will be time to plan what you might do to make the whole situation better. If there is any truth to the criticism, you can consider it and take appropriate action to apologize or fix the situation. However, in the heat of the moment, you just need to have a practical plan that will help you stay focused and intact. If you use these tools, you will find that, remarkably, the interchange often will end gracefully. Stay in the calm *I* of the hurricane, and you can communicate and respond with an open heart.

Anyone Else Think This Is A Good Idea?

When things go bad, double up your efforts on doing good…. You can turn bad news into something beautiful…. Live positive. —Craig Ballantyne

Rise above the storm and you will find the sunshine. —Mario Fernandez

If you have integrity, nothing else matters. If you don't have integrity, nothing else matters. —Alan K. Simpson

The truth is that parents are not really interested in justice. They just want quiet. —Bill Crosby

Happiness is having a large, loving, caring, close-knit family in another city. —George Burns

The best revenge is to be unlike him who performed the injury. —Marcus Aurelius

There are three sides to an argument—your side, my side, and the right side. —Unknown

My favorite:
Drawing on my fine commend of the English language, I said nothing. — Robert Benchley

Dare To Shift

Shift for general communication from the heart

Always aim to bring you closer together—this will give you immediate results!

- ♥ Will this comment or question show the openhearted and gracious person that you really are?
- ♥ If not, think of something supportive and complimentary you can say that will bring you closer!
- ♥ For any disagreement, see if both parties can agree to try listening to the other state needs and thoughts fully, without being subject to interruption, argument or attack. Then, when both of you have completely expressed yourselves, plan to work respectfully together to agree, meet in the middle, or agree to disagree.

- ♥ There is "magic in a word of praise"—give at least one compliment or positive statement every day, without fail. This is important for any business relationship. This is vital for family and partner relationships! And don't forget to connect to love for a few minutes every day, as it is the most important shift of all!

Shift for handling attack and criticism

Always aim to get through this with both of you whole and unhurt. If you are face to face, use the following techniques and examples to deal with distraction, attack, criticism, or accusation. You will feel better about yourself and get better results.

Distraction

Sometimes when you try to talk to someone or make a request, you will be met with distraction or accusation. This is often an attempt to avoid an unpleasant topic by pushing your buttons. Keep on track, and don't be distracted or defend yourself. For your own self-esteem, be kind and courteous and take the high road. The following offers examples of helpful responses to distraction:

- ♥ Distraction: "There you go again, harping on that, when I want to discuss our trip next week."
- ♥ Response: "I know you want to discuss the trip, and we can later, but I need to know when you will have money for your half of the rent. The rent is due on Monday." (ignores inflammatory word *harping* and distraction of trip topic)
- ♥ Distraction: "I know you wanted me to mow the lawn and move the garbage cans, but what about Marc and Julie? They never do their chores."
- ♥ Response: "I appreciate your concern, but whether you get to use the car this weekend will depend on you alone, so let's go over your plan now." (ignores reference to Marc and Julie)

Accusation

Do not engage with the personal attack. Always acknowledge the upset (feelings), but ignore distracting accusations. Keep the focus on the topic—do not be pushed into dropping your purpose and defending yourself.

- ♥ Attack: "I hate you, Dad! You are totally unfair! You enjoy ruining my life!"
- ♥ Response: "I would be upset about losing my car privileges, if I were you. I know it's hard. Right now I need to get your agreement to be home by eleven o'clock tonight." (Acknowledges feelings, finds point of agreement, stays on task)
- ♥ Attack: "There hasn't been a home-cooked meal around here for weeks!"
- ♥ Response: "You have a point, I have not been cooking as much lately. Since I started school, I have felt so tired. What do you think we could do differently?"
(Finds point of agreement, avoids guilt and defensiveness, and stays on task)

Sarcasm, hurtful criticism

There is no way to win against these types of comments, so refuse to argue, take the bait, or react with anger or hurt. When you react, you just perpetuate the unhappy situation, and everyone loses. These tools will help if your friend or family member is just thoughtless. The person may not realize how the critical comments hurt, or may have made the comments just to get your attention and a reaction, even if it is negative.

- ♥ At a calm time, tell your family member or friend that their comments hurt you.
- ♥ Then say, "That could hurt" when they say something you feel is hurtful. Say it every time, but say or do nothing else. (This may be the hardest part—but try it! What you have been doing has not worked.) Do not justify, defend yourself, disagree with the comment, or criticize.
- ♥ In your mind, picture the comment as a dart. Know that you can step out of its path, so it can circle around and go back to the sender. Return it to sender, let it go, and be at peace. It cannot hurt you unless you decide to let it hurt.

Physical or verbal abuse

There is never an excuse or reason for physical abuse or verbal abuse, it is never your fault. No matter what you think you may have done to cause it, the abuser always has a choice: to abuse, or not. Contact your local pastor, doctor's office, employee health office, or health department for help and information. If you cannot find that easily, call 911 and ask for the local abuse hotline or office for domestic violence. You must take action to help yourself. You deserve better. You deserve help.

What Will I Get Out Of This?

In his book, *Words Can Change Your Brain*, Dr. Newberg cites studies showing that even a single negative phrase or word releases stress chemicals and can disrupt sleep, happiness and health, while a word like "peace" can induce feelings of peace and relaxation. If you learn to pause and connect to love before you criticize others and before responding to criticism or attack, you will give yourself the gift of personal peace. Argumentative and critical people won't be attracted to someone who refuses to argue or react. They will find someone else with whom to complain. Over time you will see less of this type of behavior.

- You will be behaving in a way that will make you feel good about yourself—no regret or apologizing for your part.
- You won't be as easily distracted and manipulated by others.
- You will find it easier to see that most negative behavior is about the other person and how they are feeling about their lives, and is not about you.
- You will be able to clearly see who in your life is treating you well, without wondering if you somehow caused the problem.

Pausing before you ask for what you want and before you react to others will create more peace, and the law of attraction will bring you more peaceful, happy relationships.

Recommended Resources You Might Enjoy

Carnegie Training (2004) *The 5 Essential People Skills: How to Assert Yourself, Listen to Others and Resolve Conflicts*. New York: Simon & Schuster.
Chapman, G. (2006) *Everybody Wins: The Chapman Guide to Solving Conflicts without Arguing*. UK: Tyndale Press.
Latham, G. (1990) *The Power of Positive Parenting*. Logan, UT, P & T Ink.

Newberg, A., Waldman, M. (2013) *Words Can Change Your Brain: 12 Conversation Strategies to Build Trust, Resolve Conflict, and Increase Intimacy*. NY, Penguin Books

Picquette, E. (2012) "About Children," "About Teenagers." and "About Your Worth" on *Mini Meditation—Lighten Your Heart*—MP3's available for download

For an easy click on book list of all the reference books – go to <u>AdvisorIsIn.com</u>

Shift Key 10: Love So It Can Be Felt

Hope inspired, To love and be loved is to feel the sun from both sides. —David Viscott

Impatience—if she existed—inspired, If love is the answer, could you please rephrase the question? —Lily Tomlin

Congratulations; you have given up, released, and let go of a lot of heaviness! Your heart should feel lighter. Now it is time for more fun and creativity. It is time to open your heart again, and add even more love. Shift Key 10 includes some practical ways to enrich love relationships and add even more joy and high-vibration energy to your life. Though you are not responsible for anyone's happiness but your own, behaving with love toward yourself and toward others will make you feel great. When it is within your power, it is wonderful to give. It always adds to your own happiness if you can offer some extra pleasure or happy experience to someone else's life.

Since I spent so much of my time working on my own relationships and observing those of my friends, I noticed that many of us didn't seem to be very successful at giving love or getting the demonstrations of love for which we longed. We gave love that didn't seem to be appreciated. Our partners seemed clueless, as well. Once I began to study neuro-linguistic programming, I could see why. I learned that most of us were giving what we wanted to receive, or what we thought others expected—not what they really wanted. I learned that if we cared to find out what makes our partner or family members feel most loved, we would be more successful at showing our love and at giving meaningful gifts and experiences.

You probably learned that love and affection should be given or received in certain ways. This knowledge is usually learned from your family or observing how you wished your family behaved! Here are some examples of what you might have learned about how to express love.

- ♥ Dad always bought flowers to Mom. Dad brought presents home when he went on business. Mom always buys us clothes to show her love.
- ♥ There was always a lot of hugging and kissing at our house—we felt secure. Or, my grandma hugged us, but that's not how our house was: my mom didn't touch us much.
- ♥ Mom made Dad's favorite steak and potatoes when she was happy. My older sister always bakes our favorite dinner or cake when we come home.
- ♥ Dad showed he cared by always doing little handyman jobs around the house or building something for us.
- ♥ Mom and Dad spent special time with us, or took each of us on a special outing every birthday, doing just what we liked.

Another way to look at this is that most of us use representational systems to learn and to "decode" love. These examples are taken from neuro-linguistic programming.

- ♥ Visual—we need to see evidence: a smile, a real handwritten note in the Valentine card, the flowers, or the desired gift.
- ♥ Auditory—we need to hear the words: how we are loved; phone calls just to say hello; sincere compliments, particularly in front of friends.
- ♥ Kinesthetic: we need loving touch: hand-holding, hugging, pats, kisses, and, particularly, extra affection outside the sexual relationship.
- ♥ Gustatory, olfactory: we love fragrant flowers, perfume, aftershave; we crave chocolate, barbeque, grilling onions, the warmth of smelling cinnamon rolls or pumpkin pie.
- ♥ Time together—all of the above: seeing, hearing, touching, and most of all, undivided attention.
- ♥ Receiving a present—not what we think we should have or want, but what we really want.
- ♥ Receiving a labor of love—something we have said we want

I know a couple where each partner seems unaware of the other's need for demonstrations of love. The wife would love to have some expensive jewelry from her husband, just like the jewelry all her friends display. He doesn't believe in putting money into jewelry. He doesn't mind if she buys her own, but it is against his principles to spend his money that way. He really loves home cooking: mashed potatoes and gravy, meatloaf, homemade pies and cinnamon rolls like his grandmother made. His wife is a great cook but stopped cooking after a few years of marriage. They go out a lot, and he eats a lot of cereal. I am sure that they express their love for each other in many ways, and these are very minor things. But both partners sometimes mention what they are missing when they are talking with others. How easy it would be for them to occasionally meet each other's needs—if they were more aware of the impact.

Why does this happen, when relationships seem so promising in the beginning? I believe that neglecting the little attentions that make our partners or family members happy causes small resentments and feelings of neglect that grow over time. Most romantic relationships start out using all the ways of expression—time together, giving gifts, compliments, planning special meals and rituals, and lots of physical affection. This way, no matter the love system, usually both partners are getting their needs met. Both are sure they are a love match, and each believes the other "gets" what makes him or her happy. But as partners get comfortable in the relationship, both givers tend to cut back to their own respective preferred, easiest, or most familiar ways of showing affection. No wonder relationships wither! Most partners are giving the kinds of affection or caring that they either would want to get, or they have seen in their families. However, they are often wrong. Both partners are giving something, but they are not giving what their partners need to feel loved.

Interestingly, this seems to be true in parent-child relationships, as well. Most parents start out having this close affectionate relationship with small children, and it also gradually changes over time. Kids grow up and start being more difficult and independent. Teenagers can be rejecting—and if the parent is not solid in their own self-esteem, the parent can react by withdrawing affection. It is easy to stop giving the hugs and affection. Tweens and teens do need to grow up and attach to their friends, but even if they seem independent or even embarrassed by attention, they still need compliments, loving praise, approval, and age-appropriate hugs from their parents. In fact, they probably need it most when they appear the least lovable.

Most people—possibly including our partners and children—do not get enough *physical or verbal affection* and are starved for it. Virginia Satir, one of the originators of family therapy, said:

- ❤ "We need 4 hugs a day for survival. We need 8 hugs a day for maintenance. We need 12 hugs a day for growth."
- ❤ "I believe the greatest gift I can conceive of having from anyone is to be seen by them, heard by them, to be understood and touched by them"

When you begin expressing more affection and using the primary systems of those you love (not the representational systems that make you feel most loved), you will feel a shift toward even happier relationships. Here are some examples to help make it clear.

Love Communication Styles/Systems

Harry and Louise

- Harry is auditory: he likes to hear that he is appreciated. Louise is kinesthetic—she needs touch.
- Harry says, "I love you" frequently.
- Louise feels neglected because Harry never kisses her or hugs her outside the bedroom.
- She would love to hold hands in the movies sometimes. She would love to have him to hug her before he leaves for work and when he comes home.
- Harry says it just isn't his style. Isn't it enough that he comes home every night and takes her out to dinner often?

Joan and Mike

- Joan is very frugal with money, even though she and Mike are comfortable, middle-class professionals.
- Mike loves steak and remembers his mother's chocolate-chip cookies and apple pie with great pleasure, but Joan never fixes them. Steak is too expensive. Pie is too fattening. She does not mind making cookies, but one of the children does not like chocolate very well, so she always makes oatmeal cookies.
- Joan is affectionate, and Mike appreciates that very much. However, Mike still has a little wistfulness and wonders if he is important to Joan or if she really knows him or cares.

Sandra and Bill

- Sandra loves attention, and her father spent time listening to her talk and always brought her presents when he returned from a trip.
- Bill is visual and is always busy working on something to make their home and yard beautiful. He grew up poor, with lots of disorder and chaos. A visually beautiful home makes him feel secure.
- Bill never buys "useless" presents or gifts, and he doesn't take time to watch TV or chit-chat with Sandra. He feels Sandra should appreciate all the time he spends working for them.
- Sandra doesn't really care about all the home improvements. She just wants Bill to spend more time with her, talk with her, and maybe remember her and buy her a small gift sometimes.

Anyone Else Think This Is A Good Idea?

Affection is responsible for nine-tenths of whatever solid and durable happiness there is in our lives.
—C.S. Lewis

Those who bring sunshine into the lives of others cannot keep it from themselves. —James M. Barrie

There is no remedy for love but to love more.
   —Henry David Thoreau

Children need love, especially when they don't deserve it. —Unknown

The deepest craving of human nature is the need to be appreciated. —William James

There are two things people want more than money and sex … recognition and praise. —Mary Kay Ash

You will find as you look back upon your life that the moments when you have truly lived are the moments when you have done things in the spirit of love. —Henry Drummond

It is one of the most beautiful compensations in life … that no man can sincerely try to help another without helping himself. —Ralph Waldo Emerson

Joy boomerangs, do something for someone else … the good you do boomerangs back to you! Vicki Hitzges

And my favorite:
I must be wishing on someone else's star because someone else is always getting what I wished for. Unknown

Dare To Shift

Shift to give and receive love in the ways it can be felt and understood. Use the primary representational systems of those you love. What do they like and really want? Ask your partner or family member what makes them feel most loved and appreciated. Correct your assumptions, if necessary. You can use all the representational systems to show your love, but make sure you use their primary systems—the ones that make them feel most loved. Make a real effort to give them the kind of love and appreciation they most enjoy on a regular basis.

- ♥ Appreciate your partner or family member when you receive their love and attention, particularly when they use the representational systems that make you feel the most loved.
- ♥ Whatever their representational systems, try to include daily hugs with those you love—for your health and theirs.
- ♥ Whatever their representational systems, try to find something daily to sincerely appreciate or praise in your partner and children. Remember—there is magic in a word of praise!

Shift to reward yourself. Think about what you would like the most and what makes you feel most loved.

- ♥ Tell your partner what representational systems are most important to you—and (without criticism or blame) ask for that for yourself.
- ♥ A partner who wants the best for you will likely want to give in return. If they don't, you can decide how important it is, and whether this is one small problem in a great relationship, or if this is an indication of an unhappy or unhealthy relationship.
- ♥ But don't wait on someone else to catch on and give to you! That leads to the low energy of resentment and sadness.
- ♥ No matter what your partner does, use your knowledge to reward yourself and make your own life happy.
- ♥ If you love flowers, buy some for you! If you want to go on a trip—take yourself.

Shift to attend to what is really most important. Think about what you would do if you had only a few days or hours left with those you love—then live each day giving the love and attention you would give if you knew you didn't have forever to show your love. Treat yourself in the same loving way. If your time on earth were limited, what would you wish you had done? Do it now. Make the time and effort to love yourself and others today. And don't forget to connect to love for a few minutes every day, as it is the most important shift of all!

What Will I Get Out Of This?

Loving yourself and loving others will always be rewarded and rewarding. Give yourself the things that make you feel loved, even if you don't always get them from others. You must fill your own heart before you can pour love into anyone else. Without sacrificing yourself, give the people who are in your life all the love and affection that you reasonably can, and it will come back to you multiplied many times over. But do not look for a direct return! It may not come directly from the person you have treated lovingly, but it will come from others. Nothing can stop it. Start looking for opportunities!

- ❤ Could your boss, employees, friends, grocery clerk, or bank attendant use a sincere compliment?
- ❤ Can you find something wonderful about your partner, child, or teen to praise—every day?
- ❤ Did your partner, children, and family get their hugs from you today?

Give with an open heart, and then expect the universe to send it back to you. It will come—possibly in a different way or from someone you didn't expect. But love always comes back to the sincere giver!

Recommended Resources You Might Enjoy

Chapman, G. (1992) *The Five Love Languages*, Chicago, Northfield.

Jeffers, S. (2001) *I'm OK, You're A Brat! : Setting the Priorities Straight and Freeing You From the Guilt and Mad Myths of Parenthood*, Los Angeles: Renaissance Books.

———. (1990) *Opening Our Hearts to Men*. NY, Random House.

Newberg, A., Waldman, M. (2013) *Words Can Change Your Brain: 12 Conversation Strategies to Build Trust, Resolve Conflict, and Increase Intimacy*, NY, Penguin Books

Picquette, E. (2012) "Connecting to Love" and "Heart Blessings" on *Mini Meditation—Shift Keys,* MP3 available for download

Shimoff, M. (2010) *Love for No Reason,* NY, Simon & Schuster.

For an easy click on book list of all the reference books – go to AdvisorIsIn.com

Conclusion

Thank you for spending time with the lovely angels of inspiration, **Hope** and **Impatience** – and with me!

You know that angels can appear any way they choose. They usually appear in a way that comforts and encourages us. I believe that **Hope** and **Impatience** enjoyed seeing their portraits, even though I know they are filled with much more translucent love and light than we will ever have the ability to portray. It has been such a pleasure and comfort in my life to know that angels have been with us down through the ages – that angels are everywhere, ready to lift us up and inspire all that is good and true.

I hope you have enjoyed the journey through the 10 Shift Keys and that you have Dared to Shift in ways that lightened your heart. If you have, you should find yourself more able to live the Prayer of St. Francis.

> *Lord, make me an instrument of your peace.*
> *Where there is hatred, let me sow love.*
> *Where there is injury, pardon.*
> *Where there is doubt, faith.*
> *Where there is despair, hope.*
> *Where there is darkness, light.*
> *Where there is sadness, joy…*

Remember that you have freedom of choice – take action now to be the person you would be if you really loved yourself! Angels are all around you, wanting to inspire you and help you go toward what nourishes your relationships and delights your heart. You can connect to light and love at any time – but you hold the Shift Keys!!

- ❤ **Impatience** leaves you with this reminder - If you do not change direction, you may end up where you are heading. Lau Tzu
- ❤ **Hope** offers this soft encouragement - You are braver than you believe, and stronger than you seem, and smarter than you think. A.A. Milne

I will close with my favorite quote on change - Lord, where we are wrong, make us willing to change; where we are right, make us easy to live with. Peter Marshall

If you enjoyed this book, I would love to have you leave a review online where you purchased the book. You are also invited to visit my author page - <https://www.amazon.com/author/eve-advisorisin>, Facebook at AdvisorIsIn and my page at AdvisorIsIn.com where I offer advice and techniques to help you open your heart for the happiest relationships and life. You will also find a book list of the references in this book - and Free Angel Readings and other **Gifts** – click on Angel Messages!

And don't forget to try MP3's available for download:
Mini Meditations – Shift Keys - Open Your Heart for Happy Relationships and
Mini Meditations – Lighten Your Heart- series of 6 Mini-Meditations